The Jewish Role in American Life

An Annual Review

The Jewish Role in American Life

An Annual Review

Volume 2

Barry Glassner

Hilary Taub Lachoff

Gene Lichtenstein

USC Casden Institute for the Study of the Jewish Role in American Life
Los Angeles

ISBN 0-9717400-1-1

Book design by John Banner.
Set in Times New Roman.
Printed on Cascade 60 lb. offset.

Printed in the United States of America by
KNI, Incorporated, Anaheim, California.

Published by the USC Casden Institute for the Study of the
Jewish Role in American Life
University of Southern California,
Grace Ford Salvatori Hall, Room 304,
Los Angeles, California 90089-1697

Contents

Acknowledgements

This volume represents the collaborative efforts of many people, over many months. We would like to expressly thank a few of these individuals, without whom this project would not have been possible. First, we'd like to thank Alan Casden for his generous support of this publication and the Casden Institute for the Study of the Jewish Role in American Life. We also thank the members of the Casden Institute Advisory Board, many of whom were founding members, and all of whom advise and support the Casden Institute in each of our efforts. They are: Lewis Barth, Mark Benjamin, Joseph Bentley, Alan Berlin, Jonathan Brandler, Michael Diamond, Solomon Golomb, Jonathan Klein, Ray Kurtzman, Susan Laemmle, Beth Meyerowitz, Michael Renov, Cara Robertson, Chip Robertson, Carol Brennglass Spinner, Scott Stone, Bradley Tabach-Bank, Ruth Weisberg, and Ruth Ziegler. We'd like to thank the University of Southern California, USC President Steven B. Sample, Provost Lloyd Armstrong and Joseph Aoun, Dean of the USC College of Letters, Arts and Sciences for their continued support and for providing the intellectual and cultural environment in which we thrive. Finally, thanks to graduate students Christopher Walters and Elisabeth Finch for copy editing, recent USC graduate Marc Korman for research assistance, Kathie Bozanich for proofreading and editing, Susan Wilcox for Development operations, and Martha Harris for excellent editorial suggestions.

Introduction

It took American Jews from 1900 to 1970 to move from the position of outsider in the United States to that of insider. Flash forward a few decades and it has become difficult to identify a field of endeavor that has not been profoundly influenced by the achievements of Jewish Americans. Education, law, science, the arts and domestic and international politics are influenced by American Jews, a group that numbers only 5.2 million in a country of 280 million people.

Despite their modest population, Jews have made substantial contributions as practitioners and researchers, innovators and creators, teachers and leaders in the United States' major institutions. We began to examine and document that reality a year ago, in the first volume in this series of annual scholarly reports. In this second volume, we continue our analysis by focusing on the dialogue among different groups of Jews that has come to define the present moment in the Jewish community. That dialogue, which scholars, critics and community leaders broadly label as the search for Jewish identity, engages us in a dynamic, ever-evolving way almost every day.

Identity concerns are at the very core of scholarly inquiry at the Casden Institute for the Study of the Jewish Role in American Life, whose mission is to support research and programming that can yield insights and understanding about what it means to be Jewish in America. Each volume in this annual series attempts to further that mission by reviewing recent scholarly books, articles and critical pieces from popular publications that elucidate the current role and contributions of American Jews in five key areas: values, politics, education, image and culture.

Within those general areas, we have chosen in the second volume to concentrate our attention on biomedical ethics, international politics, experiential education, the art world, and cinema. As will become clear in the discussions that follow, our decision to focus on these areas for the 2003 volume has been influenced by recent international events and developments in scholarly literature.

We begin with a chapter in which we explore Jewish values and, more specifically, Jewish responses to recent developments in biomedical ethics. With cloning and stem-cell research, it could now feasibly be said that science fiction has become fact. Are these techniques ethically acceptable advancements, or do they enter an area that could potentially undermine our humanity or religious beliefs? These issues are of interest to many groups in the United States and internationally, but we focus primarily on the Jewish response to these ethical questions.

That discussion takes a historical look at the field of biomedical ethics and the events that incited its development—namely, the Holocaust and unethical medical experiments in the United States. The field of biomedical ethics is presently thriving, and we examine the impact of this evolution on the medical field as a whole. Jewish biomedical ethics has developed as a subset of the larger field, and its practitioners apply Jewish teachings to the questions and conflicts at hand. Issues such as abortion, stem-cell research, and cloning relate in important ways to religious teachings, and thus, part of our discussion focuses on *halachic* instruction and the Noahide laws. Specifically, we look at the place religion has been granted in these debates, and its relevance to issues such as euthanasia. How important a role has religion played in these debates, and how important *should* that role be?

In the chapter on politics, we thought it fitting, in the wake of the September 11, 2001 terrorist attacks and recent developments in the Middle East, to examine the history of the relationship between the United States and Israel and the role that American Jews have played in the development of that affiliation. The political connection between the two nations, while generally solid and strong, has varied over the years as different American presidents have shifted course on domestic politics and America's perceived foreign policy interests. These modifications in policy have been subjected to political pressures from a range of interest groups in the United States, including Jewish groups.

In our chapter on politics, we also take a look at the decline of Jewish identification through the 1990s, a trend that some blame on the political divisions within sectors of American and international Jewish communities. Despite this shift, Jews have continued to affect the United States government and have helped contribute to the sense that the interests of the United States and Israel are, more often than not, aligned.

The following chapter explores the state of Jewish education in our country. A continuing emphasis on education throughout the Jewish community is indisputable, but many scholars report a change in focus from achieving success in traditional Jewish education programs to prizing more highly the success in American education programs. Some are concerned that this change in focus coincides with a departure from Jewish values and a concomitant loss of knowledge of Jewish traditions. In this chapter, we explore experiential Jewish education as a method of revitalizing Jewish education and involving the community in making Jewish education successful, effective and meaningful for future generations.

One major component of experiential education includes programs that bring American Jews to Israel. We examine organized synagogue trips and the Birthright Israel program and the reported efficacy of these groups in conveying a tangible experience to the study of Jewish history. The research on these programs—designed to help Jews rediscover their identity and to provide a community in which to learn and encourage participants to retain community involvement after returning home—has been too limited and recent to conclude whether or not they have proved effective.

The fourth chapter scrutinizes the portrayal of Jewish life in art and artifacts. Like most explorations of this topic, ours struggles to define exactly what is meant by "Jewish art": what it is, what it is not and how Jewish artists practice it. Some Jewish American artists, such as R.B. Kitaj and Ruth Weisberg, say that their art is profoundly influenced by their Jewish character and history and cannot be viewed intelligently without considering their Jewishness. Others describe themselves as artists who happen to be Jewish.

In addition, we take a close look at the critics and art historians who kept their Jewishness apart from their interpretations of art. Also, we introduce more recent scholars who insist that it is time for Jewish art historians and art critics to acknowledge their ethnicity and examine how it affects their taste, judgment and critical analysis.

Finally, in the chapter on cinema, a more historical set of factors comes into play. We have taken note of an industry that was founded by Jewish immigrants from Eastern Europe about a century ago. The rise of those Jewish immigrants, and the entertainment world they founded, changed the images and myths that defined America. The manner in which this was accomplished helped to reshape the portrait and values of the United States.

Our chapter explores the changes that occurred in mid-century America following the decline of the studio system, the fading of studio moguls from the scene and the entrance of television into the life of the public. As Jews in the industry became more comfortable with their status and identity, the on-screen portrait of America took on a new profile, and Jews began to appear in films as characters and as actors with their own Jewish names. Some scholars interpret these changes as opening the door for a less idealized, more realistic view of American Jewry on the big and small screens. Others criticize the trend as being equally idealized, only this time screen images favor American Jews.

Taken together, these five chapters touch on some of the major contributions of Jews in our society. It was not the intention of the Casden Institute to deal with the Jewish role in its entirety; indeed, that would be impossible. Nor do we presume to publish an annual Jewish "year in review." Other sources, such as the *American Jewish Yearbook*, have been doing that for more than 100 years and there are many excellent resources available for that sort of comprehensive and statistical material. Rather, our goal for each volume is to highlight certain key factors, issues and people who receive attention in the scholarly and popular literature and to examine the elements that make these topics stand out from the rest. With a focus on contemporary scholarship and the matters that define modern Jewish living, we strive to stimulate discussion, research and further consideration of the role Jews have played and will continue to play in American life. Through our examination, it is our hope that readers may gain some insight into what it means to be Jewish in our pluralistic society.

Chapter One

VALUES:
Jewish Values in Research and Medical Ethics

N ow, perhaps more than ever before, the subject of biomedical ethics has moved to the forefront of debate and controversy in our society. Stem cell research, cloning and a score of other developments in medical science pepper the headlines on a daily basis, and questions once reserved for science fiction stories are becoming quite real and increasingly relevant in this age of information. Somewhere between the miracles of science and the cautions of critics, the question surfaces: How should one ethically respond to these innovations and breakthroughs? They offer incredible hope for our future, but also contain the possibility of an eventual moral decline.

In this chapter, we shall examine biomedical ethics (in both a modern and historical context) and its relation to our society. How has biomedical ethics transformed (and been transformed by) the practice of medicine in the United States during the past 40 years? And, what role have American Jews played in this transformation?

In order to understand a topic as complicated and all-encompassing as biomedical ethics, one must examine its history. Ethics in medical research has been controversial since 1933 when many doctors in Nazi Germany became complicit partners in state-sanctioned experiments on, and the torture and murder of, innocent citizens, many of them Jews. The doctors peformed the experiments willingly, believing that the world must be saved from the inferior races that were threatening to contaminate it. While Jewish doctors were dismissed from practicing medicine, many of the Nazi physicians remaining took part in forced sterilization programs and, eventually, state-mandated euthanasia.

These atrocities were not limited to Nazi Germany, however; the United States had its own history of experiments performed on humans without their consent. Forced sterilization laws were passed in the United States as early as 1907. Later, experiments were performed on prisoners, military personnel and even hospital patients. In addition, after the second world war, Nazi doctors condemned for their actions in the Holocaust came to America to oversee some of the United States government's experiments. In fact, the demand for a new system of biomedical ethics in which the individual rights of the patient came first stemmed from the unethical conduct discovered in our own country after World War II. Early biomedical ethicists—philosophers, lawyers, doctors and scientists—upended the practice of medicine, shifting it from what its critics deemed an authoritarian, paternalistic system to one of individualism. They paved the way for modern-day ethicists who would be forced to deal with a host of new moral quandaries.

While informing a medical subject of any potential risks involved in experimentation and obtaining consent are cardinal rules today, the path to these seemingly indelible tenets was long, complicated and far from certain. Furthermore, these guidelines, while commonplace in America and most other developed countries, are virtually non-existent in many developing nations, even today. The Holocaust in all its horrors may have been the first indication that a system of biomedical ethics was necessary, but as we will see, it has not been the last.

We shall next consider medical morality in a contemporary setting, specifically Jewish approaches and values within the context of American biomedical ethics. While the issues may have changed over the past 70 years, the underlying conflict has not.

Since the 1960s, the field of biomedical ethics has been steadily expanding. When the government's role in questionable testing procedures became common knowledge, the politically active public of the 1960s and '70s mobilized. The Hastings Center in Garrison, New York, and Kennedy Institute of Ethics at Georgetown University, institutions that would become the leaders of the field, were created during this time and helped increase awareness of this little studied concept through academic conferences and symposia. The idea of patient autonomy in treatment became central to this issue, and the 1990s recognized the study of biomedical ethics as a viable professional field.

In the past decade, as medical technology has helped improve treatment, controversy has intensified, particularly over such issues as dying patients' rights and stem cell research. We will see that not all physicians support every tenet of biomedical ethics, believing, for instance, that in some cases a patient may not realize which medical approach would best serve him/her. This dispute may have arisen, in part, because of the extremely diverse background of biomedical ethicists: philosophy, medicine, law, religion, etc. These multiple backgrounds and methodologies assist in providing a comprehensive view of modern medicine, but critics argue that these "doctor watchers" lack a common set of professional standards.

Amidst the strife, American Jews have emerged as some of the more prominent ethicists in the nation, and religion has come to play a role in the continuing development of the medical field. Jewish biomedical ethics, a subset of biomedical ethics as a whole, and Jewish Americans have become part of the decision-making process in which interest groups continue to vie for control in public policy debates. At stake is the future role of research in the American medical community. This new subspecialty in the biomedical ethics field raises a host of new questions: Do Jewish ethicists who label themselves as secularists and/or humanists draw upon their ethnic identity to inform their ethical decisions? And, what sorts of ethical considerations face Jewish physicians practicing medicine and/ or medical ethics in non-Jewish institutions? We will examine the role of religion in the public domain and the public policy issues that ethicists address.

One subject that we will explore in this chapter is the effort by Jewish philosophers, research scientists and medical doctors to integrate biomedical ethics with Jewish law. To accomplish this, we will examine several specific instances in which Jewish scholars say that the ethical concerns of today have a basis in *halachic* laws which have previously been addressed: manipulating life, decisions about death and third party requirements beyond patient rights. Does *halacha*, the Jewish code of ethics, have any relevance to modern-day biomedical ethics for Jews as some suggest? Does it have any relevance for non-Jews? The arguments are far from conclusive.

Religion has inarguably been a political factor in biomedical ethics since the field's inception and continues to play an important role, as evidenced by the fact that religious thinkers and consultants have been appointed to government commissions dealing with biomedical ethics. How does the separation of church and state play into this controversy? Some suggest that all religions are in line with basic aspects of the human condition. Thus, these ethicists feel comfortable speaking in commonly accepted secular terms. Others suggest that secular theories differ distinctly from *halachic* principles. This view is illustrated by the fact that secularists emphasize a patient's autonomous rights, while Jewish ethicists, who adhere to traditional religious law, seek fulfillment through obedience. It is clear that religion is linked to biomedical ethics, whether directly or indirectly, but the prevailing purpose of biomedical ethics is concerned with deducing universal principles of common morality. We will explore whether this secular approach can be reconciled with the religious views held almost universally by biomedical ethicists who are religious Jews.

To further illuminate this issue, we will examine the stem cell controversy and the Jewish response. Central to this topic is the question, "When does life begin?" Christian and Jewish doctrines differ significantly on this point, which plays into the conflict; and many bioethicists believe the Jewish imperative to heal overrides other concerns. The related issue of cloning also will be examined. It—cloning—appears to be a controversy in which science and politics are equally present.

The Complicity of Physicians

When the British naturalist Charles Darwin expounded his theory of natural selection in *On the Origin of Species* in 1859, many Western philosophers and thinkers realized something quite daring and different had occurred: Our perception of life on the planet had been altered. It took several decades before some of the applications of Darwin's theory were shifted from nature and animal life to a focus on man. Some scientists and social theorists saw a connection between Darwin's theory about the survival of the fittest and a process of selective breeding in humans. This belief that society could be improved through eugenics, or the science of selective breeding, soon developed a following in Germany, where social scientists and doctors were "concerned about what they saw as a dark side to the industrial age and worried that degradation of the human species was occurring" (Geiderman 224). They proclaimed inferior races were beginning to dominate the population at the expense of pure Nordic Aryans. Medical care might benefit individuals, according to German social Darwinists of the late 19th and early 20th centuries, but it was pulling down society as a whole by preserving and extending the lives of those deemed less fit and racially pure.

The Nazis took power in 1933 and social Darwinist doctrine became a form of applied biology that was put into practice. Its most enthusiastic participants were Germany's doctors, many of whom rushed to become members of the Nazi Party and, in some cases, officers in the SS. Jewish physicians (who constituted from 13 percent to 17 percent of the doctors in Germany and from 50 percent to 60 percent specifically in Berlin) were dismissed from their posts at hospitals (Geiderman 225). The eugenics movement became linked to Nazi philosophy and German anti-Semitism. In July 1933, Germany's National Socialists enacted the Law for the Prevention of Hereditarily Diseased Descendents (the Sterilization Act). It stated that anyone deemed to be carrying genetically based diseases could be sterilized, including "the feebleminded, manic depressives, people with serious deformities, such as congenital deafness or blindness," and alcoholics. "The law required the surgical sterilization of 50,000 individuals annually" (Geiderman 226). Doctors became willing accomplices, reporting with or without consent the names of patients whom they recommended for sterilization.

In short order, the practice of medicine in Nazi Germany became an arm of the state. Decisions were made allowing experiments on humans without their consent, enforced sterilization was introduced as government policy, mass extermination of those deemed to be unfit took place in national hospitals, and a policy to exclude Jewish physicians from practicing medicine was adopted by the German government and actively embraced by doctors (Geiderman 227). Under a national policy of cleansing the gene pool, German doctors cooperated in sterilizing an estimated 360,000 men and women, and killing more than 70,000 asylum inmates (Geiderman 227).

In this way, eugenics also soon led to forms of euthanasia that were prescribed by the state. The right to live had to be justified rather than assumed, and doctors were required to pass judgment on whether or not a patient should have that right. In 1939 doctors and midwives were ordered by a government committee to notify authorities of any babies born with defects. Initially, it covered children up to 3 years old, but by 1941, the euthanasia program included the option of reporting and potentially putting to death children up to 17 years of age (Geiderman 227).

The moral failure of the medical profession in Germany was not discussed. After the defeat of Germany in World War II, the Nuremberg trials revealed that thousands of physicians were implicated in the policy decisions to put to death children with birth defects. The organized medical community closed ranks to conceal the past, details of the Nuremberg findings were suppressed and physicians and scientists who wrote about it were subject to sanctions or were ostracized by professional groups such as the World Medical Organization and the West German Chamber of Physicians (Geiderman 230).

Not every doctor committed crimes, nor was everyone in the profession corrupt. But as Dr. Joel Martin Geiderman, chief of emergency medicine at Cedars-Sinai Medical Center and a respondent in the Jewish Values and Medicine Conference co-sponsored by Cedars Sinai and the Casden Institute in October 2001, stated: "What is worthy of pondering is how *any* doctor could have acted in such a manner" (Geiderman 230).

Unfortunately, unethical conduct by those in the medical field was not limited to Nazi Germany. Early in the 20th century, eugenics had followers and enthusiasts in many countries, including the United States (Shannon 1-3). Sterilization programs were undertaken in the United States, Switzerland, Norway and Sweden. In 1907, the first law authorizing sterilization of the mentally ill and the criminally insane was approved in Indiana. Twenty-eight other states followed suit, leading to the sterilization of 15,000 American men and women by 1930 (Geiderman 226).

During World War II, the United States government, under the banner of serving the interests of national security, conducted biochemical experiments on prisoners of war and criminals who were incarcerated, as well as on civil service employees, hospital patients and military personnel. The government did not seek consent (http Amazon Rev. of *Undue Risk...*). From the standpoint of those conducting the experiments, the need to know the results outweighed the rights of the individuals.

After World War II, populations from Utah to Alaska became unwitting subjects for test releases of radioactive substances. The United States Air Force conducted experiments on 253 patients from 1951-56 "to test exposure levels for their proposed nuclear powered aircraft," resulting in nausea, vomiting and death (Shannon 2). Military personnel participated in experiments as well. They were viewed as a "captive" population, and more than 65,000 were used as subjects in experimental chemical programs. For example, sailors were selected to sit in gas chambers that had been filled with mustard gas until they passed out (Shannon 2). Prisoners were tricked into volunteering for testicle irradiation in experiments funded by the Atomic Energy Commission. Those who volunteered for gonorrhea and malaria experiments in the 1940s were offered $100 "and were led to believe it would result in leniency when parole time came" (Shannon 2). The United States government brought in 1,600 Nazi scientists condemned at Nuremberg to help supervise the experiments (Shannon 3).

Dr. Jonathan Moreno has examined the ethical conflict surrounding this research in his book *Undue Risk: Secret State Experiments on Humans*. Moreno, a professor of biomedical ethics at the University of Virginia and a former member of the Advisory Committee on Human Radiation Experiments during the Clinton administration, found that the United States government had engaged in secret experiments on human subjects in 1945 by injecting them with plutonium (Flynn 4). He discussed his research findings in Los Angeles in October 2001 at the Jewish Values and Medicine conference co-sponsored by Cedars-Sinai and the Casden Institute. Moreno based much of his research on personal interviews, government documents that he was able to examine as a member of the advisory committee and earlier investigations. His book details the behind-the-scenes struggle over medical ethics and the government's "often half-hearted attempt to impose guidelines on human experimentation" (Flynn 4).

The problem is less about corruption than about misplaced bureaucratic zeal and priorities that elevate the perception of national security above all else. Moreno has written: "A paradox of human experiments is that they often must be done to learn about the dangers of some agents, in spite of the general ethical obligation not to expose people to harm" (Flynn 4). The consequences of this dilemma were that subjects were not always informed of an experiment's risks, nor was consent universally sought. These tenets—informing a subject of risk and obtaining consent—have become the cardinal rules governing experiments on humans.

Today, it is illegal to experiment on children in the United States. Since 1970, wide-scale experimentation on prisoners has ended, and the Army says its testing is done only for defense purposes. However, other countries have not made the strides in this area that America has. Recently, physicians in Afghanistan during the Taliban's rule were reported to have participated "in the deliberate maiming of prisoners before a crowd of spectators in a soccer stadium" (Geiderman 230). Also, genocidal actions by doctors have been recorded in Argentina, Bosnia, Croatia and Rwanda in recent years (Geiderman 230).

The action of some doctors and research scientists illuminates at least one reason the field of biomedical ethics came into existence in the years after the defeat of Nazi Germany and the onset of the Cold War. There was the recognition, at least on the part of some, that ethical guidelines and standards of practice guaranteeing the rights of patients needed to be articulated and adopted by the medical profession. Today, these biomedical ethical ideals—autonomy, beneficence, non-maleficence, justice and confidentiality, all ignored or nonexistent under the terms of the Sterilization Act in Germany—have become an integral part of medical practice.

The Evolution of a New Field in Medicine

During the past 40 years, a new approach to medical practice and an entirely new field, biomedical ethics, has evolved in the United States. In part, as stated earlier in this chapter, this has been a response to the medical practices of German doctors during the war. Also, it has been based on the rapid changes in medical technology and the social upheavals that occurred in American society in the 1960s. These historical factors helped bring about a radical shift within the practice of medicine. Biomedical ethicists have described this shaping of current medical ethics as "a shift in the physician-patient relationship from the primacy of beneficence and paternalism to the primacy of autonomy" (http "Why Jewish Medical Ethics?" 1). During the past two decades, biomedical ethicists have presided over the changed agenda in medical care and "autonomy, self-determination and legal right to privacy have become overriding principles." These values have been accompanied by an emphasis "on individual liberty" (http "Why Jewish Medical Ethics?" 1).

One result of this shift in priorities "has been to undermine the 2,500-year-old Hippocratic model of the physician as the benign, authoritarian, paternalistic decision-maker, taking full responsibility for the welfare of the patient" (http "Why Jewish Medical Ethics?" 1). Awareness has led to more public involvement in the medical decision-making process, and this in turn has helped further the individual rights of patients. This focus on patients' rights has been enhanced by continuous and prominent media coverage and dramatization on popular television programs. These issues and conflicts are today widely deliberated at state and federal levels, "in the courts and in government committees and legislatures" (Messikomer 1). One practical result is that today doctors are compelled not only to avoid harming patients, but also to gain informed consent for a specific course of treatment (Satel and Stolba 2).

While many doctors welcomed the shared responsibility in making decisions and, in some cases, the relief from the threat of medical liability in legal disputes, not all doctors greeted the role of biomedical ethics with enthusiasm (Satel and Stolba 4). In some instances, the consequences have been troubling when consent of the patient has been given precedence. One case involved a mentally disturbed patient who sawed off his hand and then refused to permit doctors to reattach it. Patient consent prevailed over medical response, and some doctors felt that the emphasis on individual autonomy in this instance proved harmful and was detrimental to the relationship between physician and patient (Satel and Stolba 3).

In the mid-1970s, newspapers publicized the case of Karen Ann Quinlan, a young New Jersey woman who was being kept alive on a respirator. The physician insisted she be artificially sustained; the woman's father sought relief from the courts. Eventually, the state's Supreme Court ruled in favor of the father (Satel and Stolba 1). The doctor's responsibility to keep the patient alive at all costs had been overruled, and the government had ratified that change in policy. "Autonomy, self-determination and legal right to privacy had become overriding principles" (http "Why Jewish Medical Ethics? " 1).

In theory, the ancient Hippocratic oath, "with its pledge to 'come for the benefit of the sick' and to refrain from divulging the confidences of patients or engaging in sexual relations with them" (Satel and Stolba 1) is still passed along in some form to the students of most medical schools. But Hippocrates said little about granting rights to a patient, according to the early biomedical ethicists in the 1960s.

The concern of some medical activists, mainly legal scholars, philosophers, social scientists and physicians, helped a new field to evolve. Along with this came a new specialist, the biomedical ethicist who was soon included within such public policy organizations as the National Institutes of Health and the Public Health Service and as advisors on congressional health committees. They became staff members or consultants in clinics, hospitals and managed-care companies (Satel and Stolba 1).

Scholarly conferences were held, symposia were conducted in scholastic and foundation settings, and issues such as the rights of patients in death and dying, organ transplantation and fertility techniques became part of an academic and public discourse. The Rockefeller Foundation and National Endowment of the Humanities funded some of the first conferences and helped establish the Hastings Center for Bio-Ethics, which was headed by Daniel Callahan, a University of Chicago legal philosopher. Callahan, one of the early leaders in the biomedical ethics movement, explained that he wanted "to give philosophy 'some social bite, some relevance'" (Satel and Stolba 1). The Hastings Center program was soon followed by the establishment of the Kennedy Institute of Ethics at Georgetown University and the Society for Health and Human Values (Satel and Stolba 2).

Today, the field of biomedical ethics is booming. Biomedical ethicists have become part of the team in hospitals, on congressional committees and in universities. They function as "doctor watchers" and, at times, as patient advocates. They often are involved in making tough medical decisions, such as determining who might receive a liver transplant or whether or not aggressive measures should be taken to revive someone declared brain dead. They are "insiders" in everything from a patient's illness to decisions about a patient's fate (Satel and Stolba 2). In addition, biomedical ethics is now an active field of study at more than 50 universities. Courses are offered and journals are published, including the Journal of Clinical Ethics, the Cambridge Quarterly of Healthcare Ethics and the Hastings Center Report. By 2001, there were about 1,600 members of the American Society for Bio-Ethics and Humanities (Geiderman 2).

Initially, two new procedures introduced by the biomedical ethicists helped create the climate for change in "modern medical care" within the United States. The ethicists ensured that informed consent accompanied all medical experiments, and they insisted on determining the competency of patients. Both policies were related to the decision-making process in life-and-death problems, which had begun to attract the attention of biomedical ethicists as modern medical care became more technologically advanced and sophisticated (Satel and Stolba 1).

What had primarily been a focus for scholars and specialists soon graduated into a public concern. Information about the Nazi practices during the Holocaust had become more widespread in the 1970s as reports and accounts from survivors filtered into the social mainstream in the form of books, newsmagazine reports and television dramas. This was accompanied by further '70s-era revelations that the United States government had deliberately failed to treat hundreds of African-American sharecroppers with syphilis as part of a medical research program in Alabama (Satel and Stolba 1).

As biomedical ethics integrated into the new medical establishment, criticism was raised by skeptics who claimed that it lacked a set of professional standards. They contended that biomedical ethics had almost no core knowledge of any substance, and that, within the field, there was a lack of consensus on treatment for any specific issue (Satel and Stolba 3). One study published in the Journal of the American Medical Association followed 100 ethics consultants who were asked to review seven different, though common, medical situations. The researchers found no majority response for six of the seven examples (Satel and Stolba 3).

Part of the difficulty, apparently, stems from the diversity of training and/or background of biomedical ethicists. "Some are Ph.D.-level academics (usually in philosophy), others are lawyers, sociologists or social workers, and still others are physicians or nurses" (Satel and Stolba 3). The field has expanded to include theologians, life science academics and students in the humanities. Training varies widely, from considerable doctoral-level work to an intensive 10-day course offered by the Kennedy Institute of Ethics at Georgetown University.

Within these institutes, ethicists and doctors are trying to reconstruct the field of medicine by sorting out those elements that seem viable and rejecting the rest (http "Why Jewish Medical Ethics" 2). They recognize that changes in society, medical technology and research, as well as the relationship between physician and patient, have all led to a set of "medical-moral dilemmas" (http "Why Jewish Medical Ethics" 2). One suggested solution to the dilemma, which is dismissive of biomedical ethics, calls for the twin aspects of care-giving—treating sick patients and recognizing patient autonomy—to be reconciled within the physician. In this scenario, ethical doctors are viewed as preferable to a bifurcated system, which sets up doctors as medical technicians and biomedical ethicists as sensitive, moral decision-makers (Satel and Stolba 4).

Secular and Religious Voices

Despite the presence of theologians, modern biomedical ethics might fairly be classified as a secular discipline. Nevertheless, its rapid development has been accompanied by a separate track of "religiously based ethical inquiry, both Jewish and Christian" (Levin and Birnbaum 469). For some of the approximately nine percent of total physicians and 14 percent of psychiatrists in the

United States who are Jewish, a traditional Judaic view governs their way of dealing with medical ethics and, in a broader sense, shapes the patient-doctor relationship (Levin and Birnbaum 469).

This traditional Jewish approach to biomedical ethics is grounded in *halachic* literature and has drawn critical comments from secular practitioners, for whom this position is "narrowly structured, legalistic, authority based and, therefore, inarguable and of no moral value or appeal to the wider community" (Levin and Birnbaum 470). Observant Jewish practitioners who are not Orthodox, however, claim that their "methods, deliberations values and principles," although related to the concerns, beliefs and biomedical ethical dilemmas of observant Jews (http "Why Jewish Medical Ethics?" 2), can be relevant to all physicians (Levin and Birnbaum 470). It is important, however, to emphasize the points of difference between Orthodox practitioners and other Jewish physicians.

For traditional Jews, individual rights and preferences yield to a sense of obligations, commandments and duties. The relationship between doctor and patient is considered a covenant in Judaism, rather than a contract between free individuals like the model adopted by American Medical Association (http "Why Jewish Medical Ethics" 2-3). In the modern, secular model, the primary concern is patient autonomy, which supercedes all other values. In Judaism, while it values and respects autonomy, the emphasis is on a different order of moral conduct: the obligations of the individual and society as bound by *halacha,* which governs "the life of each individual, patient and physician alike." Autonomy is given less weight, and a paternalism based on moral-religious exigencies is reasserted (http "Why Jewish Medical Ethics" 3).

The emphasis on a religious approach is not irrelevant. Biomedical ethicists in the mid- 1960s to the early 1970s were either trained in religious philosophy or active in theology. Even those who identified themselves as secular, according to one study, had more "than a casual relationship to religion" (Messikomer 2). The issues that have dominated conferences in the past 20 years—such as abortion, assisted reproduction, organ replacement and life support for brain-dead patients—made their way into the national consciousness in the 1960s and '70s and became the concern of organized religious groups and governmental commissions. These issues had become part of a national public policy debate, and the separation of church and state became central to the dialogue (Messikomer 11).

In large measure because the courts had upheld the separation of church and state, religious scripture had to be bypassed, though prominent religious leaders were called on to give testimony. Their task was to relate religious thought to political and moral issues. Almost everyone understood this (Messikomer 11). Rabbis J. David Bleich, M. David Feldman, Immanuel Jakobovits and Seymour Siegel were some of the more prominent Jewish religious participants. Jewish biomedical ethicists tended to come from medicine and law: for example physician-scientist Leon R. Kass, who became passionately involved with the consequences of biomedical ethical issues but who described himself as a "stridently secular Jew, someone who was linked to the Jewish prophetic tradition" (Messikomer 4). Dr. Kass, who is a professor within the Committee on Social Thought at the University of Chicago, was chosen last year by President George W. Bush to head the new Council on Bio-Ethics.

Despite the public nature of the debates and the mandate to separate public policy from religion, some topics involved religious thinkers and testimony by necessity. Nevertheless, the religious scholars were generally assigned an ambiguous role as participants and consultants on government commissions. When a federal commission focused on "Research on the Fetus (1975) and Research Involving Children (1977)," religious thinkers were invited to participate as consultants and witnesses (Messikomer 12). However, the viewpoints expressed by theologians Paul Ramsey, Richard McCormick and Stanley Hauerwas were consigned to the appendices, and not the body, of the report (Messikomer 12). This became a general practice.

The inclusion of religious leaders in the Commission on Cloning was a recognition that society was dealing with something beyond science and medicine (Messikomer 14). But in the final report, the commission again emphasized that the separation of church and state should impose limits on religion's role in the debate (Messikomer 14). "Because religious traditions influence and shape the moral views of many American citizens, and religious teachings over the centuries have provided an important source of ideas and inspiration ... in a pluralistic society, particular religious views cannot be determinative for public policy decisions that bind everyone" (Messikomer 15). Ultimately, religious thinking played largely a procedural role in congressional committee hearings and commission reports, which made the final decisions politically acceptable (Messikomer 16).

Religious thinking may have been consigned to the footnotes and appendices of commission and conference reports, but the writings of religious ethicists, particularly those who are Jewish, have played a prominent part in the discussion of issues in biomedical ethics. For example, several Jewish writers have provided a Jewish perspective on stem-cell research, including *Pioneers in Jewish Medical Ethics* by Dr. Fred Rosner; *Duty and Healing: Foundation of a Jewish Bio-Ethic* by Dr. Benjamin Freedman; *Healthcare and the Ethics of the Encounter* by Laurie Zoloth, Ph.D.; and *Matters of Life and Death*: A *Jewish Approach to Modern Medical Ethics* by Rabbi Elliot N. Dorff. Some of the writing is decidedly secular, but much of it emanates from a Jewish perspective and adopts a *halachic* approach. Drs. Rosner and Freedman offer a *halachic* view of how medical ethics is intertwined with Judaism, Zoloth links feminism and *halacha* in her analysis of an Oregon health-care plan, and Dorff follows a traditional Conservative line of reasoning on euthanasia, but parts with Jewish law on the issue of homosexuality (Novak 2). He gives sway, at times, to moral reasoning over tradition and disagrees with the Orthodox approach, which assigns primacy to *halacha* over all other imperatives (Novak 3).

Religious Perspectives and Biomedical Ethics

Some religious biomedical ethicists choose a rational way of resolving the church-state conflict, ultimately setting aside religious arguments. They understand that concepts of all religions are usually in line with basic aspects of the human condition, and so they assume that ethical behavior norms, known as the "the Noahide laws," can be applied to all descendants of Noah (Newman 555). Religion, in this context, is related to neither a specific doctrine nor a particular faith. It is concerned primarily with transcendent aspects of the human condition, such as questions about human origins, identity, injustice, pain and the mysteries of life and death (Messikomer 2). While the concerns are theological, the mode of discourse is secular. In this way, religious thinkers learn to screen out theological frames of reference: a recognition that in a pluralistic society, religion cannot determine public policy. Biomedical ethicists who subscribe to this view tend to check their specific religion at the door and speak in commonly accepted secular terms (Messikomer 5).

Others assume that religious thought and tradition can bring a valuable perspective to the biomedical ethical enterprise, and they actively include religious language and viewpoints in their discourse. Dr. Mark Levin, assistant professor of medicine at State University of New York's Downstate College of Medicine, and Dr. Ira Birnbaum, who is affiliated with Staten Island University Hospital's Department of Alcohol and Drug Rehabilitation, believe that *halachic* methods of inquiry can be of great value for secular ethicists (Levin and Birnbaum 472). They contend that Jewish tradition relies on texts and precedents, much like the law, to support rational arguments (Levin and Binrbaum 473). The *halachic* discourse based on critical reasoning "opens the way for a Jewish bio-ethics that is potentially relevant even for those who do not grant its basic assumptions about Divine Revelation" (Levin and Birnbaum 473).

Some critics, while agreeing that *halachic* principles relate directly to medical practice, maintain that secular theories of biomedical ethics start with the assumptions that individual rights are primary, choice rests with the patient, the arrangement between patient and doctor is contractual, and that Judaism has a somewhat different agenda, placing higher value on life and beneficence. While secularists emphasize a rights ethic, Jewish ethicists look for moral self-fulfillment through obedience or moral religious norms that are shared by all observant Jews. Given this divergence, biomedical ethics has pursued a course that continues to be steadfastly secular, with a central goal of formulating universal principles that will establish the basis for a common morality. The aim is to rise "above particulars of cultural, ethical and religious differences" (Messikomer 6).

This aim has been true almost from the very beginning. Early theoreticians of biomedical ethics emerged primarily from the academic world, trained in analytic philosophy and were complemented, at times, by the presence of legal scholars. The prevailing mode of philosophy in the 1960s and '70s was logical positivism, based on a small set of concepts and with the emphasis on precise language and systems. Religious thought, while interesting, was considered ambiguous and outside philosophical concerns.

An approach based on analytic philosophy was subsequently re-enforced as physicians and biologists joined the ranks of the biomedical ethics groups. Their concerns were also systematic and analytic. As a result, they were effective in helping steer the public debates and political deliberations that began to unfold in courts and legislatures in a functional direction (Messikomer 7).

In addition, while biomedical ethicists usually were trained to deal with issues in a systematic and analytic way, a number of those drawn to this field of study were products of their time and had some broad political experience in the civil rights and anti-war movements (Messikomer 6). The result: Most people who entered the field assumed that some form of consensus was necessary, and achievable, on most issues, and that a common morality was an end goal. Religion was not ignored; indeed, it was usually present. However, it was employed as a way of strengthening or filtering out proposals that deflected the goals of competing groups in the public arena; its role was often a political one (Messikomer 7).

Refining and Advancing the Medical Ethics Debates

Religious thinkers are aware that their struggle in biomedical ethics is mainly uphill. A secular perception of the issues, including the need to arrive at a consensual form of agreement and closure, prevails in American society today, but agreement has not been reached in many specific cases. It is with this backdrop of uncertainty that Jews and other scholars have seen an opportunity to refine and advance the contemporary debates by offering religious insights and precedents that might help illuminate issues, particularly when the ethical concerns have a basis in *halacha* or the Jewish law. In three broad areas— manipulation of life, decisions about death and dying and third-party requirements that extend beyond a patient's rights— conclusions drawn by traditional Jewish physicians and researchers may serve as guidelines for all members of our pluralistic society.

Manipulating Life

When does life begin? Different religious groups (Jews and Roman Catholics, for example), and even members within the same denomination, disagree. This dissension has led to conflict among religious groups in the political controversy over stem-cell research. Pope John Paul II and most officials in the Catholic Church assert that life commences in the embryonic tissue itself. Therefore, they call for a ban on embryo-cell research, because it results in killing a human (Maguire 1). Many of the mainstream Protestant churches share this view (Maguire 2).

Jewish understanding is somewhat different. A fetus is not viewed as an en-souled person in the Catholic sense; moreover, the "first 40 days of conception are considered 'like water' " (Maguire 2). In general, most Jews do not believe that life begins until the head appears in the process of giving birth. These conflicting perspectives have pitted Jews against Catholics and fundamental Christians. On the secular side of the debate, it has caused a split between observant and secular Jews.

A specific conflict has arisen over the findings related to genetic testing. Many American health-care providers look to genetic testing as a way to determine whether a fetus is "defective." Once the arrival of a normal healthy baby is in doubt, the decision to abort is seen by some physicians as "rational and the opportunity to do so as fortunate" (Burtt 1). It is a confirmation of individual choice and autonomy of the parent, which many Jewish physicians and health-care providers wholeheartedly support. But it is unacceptable to followers of Orthodox and Conservative Judaism.

Shelley Burtt, the parent of a child with Down syndrome has argued that the medical approach is disingenuous. It avoids the issue of curing by destroying the entity. It is, she argues, a form of eugenics, either medical through the doctor's recommendation or personal by parental choice. There is little effort to help parents understand what is involved in caring for a child with special needs and no consideration that anything positive can come from it. She raises the question: How can we predict how we as people might grow and change when faced with such adversity? What might be preferable, she argues, is to develop support with a community, which in turn might depend on teaching that community to value such children (Burtt 2-4).

Aborting a fetus diagnosed with a severe disability such as spina bifida or Down syndrome ignores the relatively high "quality of life available" to children afflicted with this disability (Burtt 3). Informed choice for prospective parents would include understanding that some lives outside the normal range are worth living and worth living with. Such a view is based on respect for all people because they are human. It stems from religious traditions that "teach us that each human life has independent and intrinsic value" (Burtt 4).

Human rights activists argue that such "freedom" of choice feeds into the international practice of "sex-selective abortions." Information from prenatal sonograms enables women to abort a female fetus in societies that value male over female children. These are unjust cultural constructions that need to be challenged, according to one critic (Burtt 3).

At times it is the method of manipulating life that poses difficult ethical choices, particularly for Jews. In vitro fertilization, for example, is science's attempt to assist couples who are infertile and wish to have children. All branches of Judaism find this acceptable. However, if multiple zygotes are implanted in the female, in vitro can yield eight embryos. At this point, parents and their doctor need to consider "carrying all the embryos to term or aborting some, a process called selective reduction" (Tenzer 1). Ethical conflicts are present in each choice. The decision to carry all embryos to term poses health risks. Terminating lands the parent in the thicket of abortion and the questions that surround it. One Reform rabbi posits that two or three zygotes might be planted into the womb at a given time. Another rabbi disagrees, saying, "if medical experts recommend not limiting the number of implanted fetuses, their advice should be heeded" (Tenzer 1). The Union of American Hebrew Congregation's Department of Jewish Family Concerns has sponsored a number of conferences dealing with infertility recently. The dilemma is clear: Jews must steer between two possibilities, individual choice on the mitzvah of having children or accepting what is permitted according to *halacha*. The religious, Jewish biomedical ethicists are concerned that parents be aware of all the implications that accompany deciding for individual choice over moral Jewish law, especially in those instances where manipulating life is at issue.

Decisions About Death

The donation of human organs is one subject Jews tend to avoid. There is the sense that it is unacceptable under Jewish law to offer up one's body after death. However, quite the reverse is true for all branches of Judaism. Indeed, the donation of a human organ is viewed as a mitzvah, because it is a quite specific way of helping to save a life. The difficulties for many Jews are ones that are seen throughout the general population: a fear of surgery, a reluctance to deal with death in advance, and vague notions about resurrection, which rest on an assumption that all body parts must be present in order to be resurrected. There is also the *halachic* concept of *kavod hamet*, "preserving the body that housed the departed soul," which comes into play (Gruenbaum Fax 2). All of these reasons help explain why the Jewish community's record of organ donations ranks among the lowest of any ethnic group (Gruenbaum Fax 1).

Part of the problem for some Jews revolves around the

halachic definition of death. "All organs from cadavers are harvested when the donor is brain dead, but machines are keeping the donor's heart and blood flowing, since organs begin to deteriorate as soon as they are deprived of oxygen" (Gruenbaum Fax 3). That is the medical field's standard definition and practice. In classic Talmudic terms, however, death occurs "when a feather held below the nose doesn't move, and when an ear pressed to the chest does not hear a heartbeat" (Gruenbaum Fax 3). Medical technology's definition becomes the source of debate. Within Reform and Conservative Judaism, Jews have been encouraged to donate their organs after death. Among Orthodox Jews, the *halachic* debates are heated (Gruenbaum Fax 3). The Rabbinical Council of America, an Orthodox umbrella group, declared in 1991 that brain-stem death fulfilled *halachic* criteria, and therefore Orthodox Jews were urged to make their organs available (Gruenbaum Fax 3). Such contributions were a way of saving lives.

But a separate Orthodox umbrella group, Agudath Israel of America, disagreed. "A beating heart renders a person living," and therefore " removing organs from a patient on a respirator constitutes murder" (Gruenbaum Fax 3). Agudath eventually decided the authority rested with the patient's rabbi, the consensus being that the donor should not put himself or herself into mortal danger (Gruenbaum Fax 3).

Jewish law and the federal law agree on the issue of physician-assisted suicide. Each prohibits it. The Supreme Court declared recently in a 9-0 decision that doctors who "prescribe life-ending drugs to mentally competent, terminally ill patients who no longer wish to live" have committed a crime (Kurtzman 1). Most segments of the Jewish community support this view. Jewish ethicists claim that a physician's primary responsibility is to work toward saving a patient's life, not ending it (Kurtzman 1). "…Doctor-assisted suicide is simply non-*halachic*; it violates a basic premise of Judaism," said Rabbi Gerald Wolpe, head of the Jewish Theological Seminary's bioethics institute (Kurtzman 1).

Not every Jewish doctor agrees. Dr. Samuel Klagsbrun, a Conservative in New York and chairman of pastoral psychiatry at the Jewish Theological Seminary, believes doctors should "be able to respond to suicide requests made by terminally ill patients" (Kurtzman 2), even though this goes against Jewish law.

Though Jewish and federal law agree on rejecting physician-assisted suicide, the same cannot be said of the debate over when brain death has occurred. The courts and some physicians have adopted what might be referred to as the secular position, a utilitarian approach that urges support for those in need of organ transplants as rapidly and safely as possible. The *halachic* view (actually views, because there is controversy among the Jewish authorities) emphasizes the need to conform to Jewish law; maintaining life until expiration has occurred is a Jewish obligation (Breitowitz "The Brain Death ..." 1).

Technological advances, such as the development of heart-lung machines and life- support respirators, have fueled this debate. When is a dying patient deemed to have expired? Only then can his or her vital organs be transplanted if permission has been granted. Secular physicians point to the scarcity of medical resources and the extensive waiting lists for organs. To facilitate transplantation, especially in life-and-death situations, the medical profession, the courts, and state legislatures have developed a definition for "brain death" that relies on neurological criteria. This is important, because hearts and livers are effective in transplants "if they are removed at a time when blood is circulating" (Breitowitz "The Brain Death..." 2). Once circulation ceases, the organ is unusable.

From a medical standpoint, the issue seems straightforward: Transplant operations are increasingly successful, giving life to patients whom otherwise might soon die. The act of sustaining a "brain dead" patient's life on the respirator, however, is increasingly seen as a useless, and expensive, medical approach. This equation has led to the decision to redefine the moment when death occurs to optimize the recovery of those who might live. As codified by law today, "death is deemed to occur when there is either irreversible cessation of circulatory and respiratory functions, or irreversible cessation of all functions of the entire brain, including the brain stem" (Breitowitz "The Brain Death..." 2).

The main purpose of the second standard is to ensure that a "comatose, ventilator-dependent patient ... whose heart is still beating due to the provision of oxygen via an artificial breathing apparatus" can be declared dead (Breitowitz "The Brain Death..." 3).

Contemporary *halachic* views are less clear and unified on this matter. Israel's Chief Rabbinate Council sought a way to coordinate its views with those of the medical majority. It authorized Hadassah Hospital to engage in heart transplant surgery but on the basis of a different set of assumptions. The council ruled that brain death was said to have occurred with the "irreversible cessation of respiration" (Breitowitz "The Brain Death..." 7). This is generally a less-exacting standard "than clinical brain death" (Breitowitz "The Brain Death..." 7) and appears more compatible with the secular-medical concept. However, the Rabbinical Council of America's *halacha* board has opposed authorizing the removal of vital organs from a patient who, while respirator dependent, has also been declared brain dead (Breitowitz "The Brain Death..." 7).

R. Moshe Feinstein, one of the leading Orthodox authorities in the United States, has adopted a more controversial stance. He has stated that removal of an organ for transplantation was murder of the donor. He opposed brain death legislation in New York unless it contained exemptions for religious reasons (Breitowitz "The Brain Death..." 6).

Beyond Patient Rights

Judaism offers insights into a patient's rights in a variety of settings, including responding to people with AIDS, dealing with informed consent and making decisions for people deemed incompetent as well as those in managed care.

The Torah mandates that both patient and disease must receive all the medical help available, regardless of the illness or its cause. This commission includes assisting people with AIDS, where a confidentiality issue also is present. AIDS patients sometimes refuse to be tested, on the grounds that confidentiality may be breached and jobs imperiled. Under Torah law, embarrassing information may not be disclosed about a person, even if the facts are accurate. This commandment is a way of constraining malicious social gossip, but it is not absolute. Negative information can be discussed in order to prevent harm from befalling others. Nondisclosure could result in the deaths of others. "*Halacha* would thus appear to support compulsory testing and mandatory disclosure" (Breitowitz "AIDS..." 3).

However, public health experts have argued that if confidentiality were guaranteed, people with AIDS would undergo testing and treatment. If the results were positive, they could then voluntarily inform others about their status and, at the very least, practice safe sex so as not to endanger others (Breitowitz "AIDS..." 3). In the long run, the pledge of absolute confidentiality is liable "to save many more lives in the future" (Breitowitz "AIDS..." 3).

Informed consent illuminates some of the differences between a secular approach to medicine and a Judaic one. The Jewish concept emphasizes obligation. The patient is obliged to become informed and must give consent for treatment if it is deemed necessary and appropriate by the physician (Eisenberg 1). When hazardous surgery is recommended, the patient must pursue answers to all the logical questions that arise, including the possibility of other options. This search is in the nature of accepting the Jewish responsibility to make an informed decision. But once all the information is collected, the patient (Eisenberg 3) must make a decision. Rabbi Moshe Feinstein has reasoned that "the patient's input is critical in medical decision-making." Coercion is advocated when the prescribed treatment is obvious and unequivocal and the patient refuses treatment. Feinstein distinguishes here between those who fear the pain that accompanies treatment and those who distrust the doctor's judgment (Eisenberg 2). The former must be persuaded to give consent, the latter to find a different physician (Eisenberg 3).

Making Decisions for Those Deemed Incompetent

The duty of Jewish children to their parents is not clearly defined by simply falling back on rituals or *halacha* expressed in Exodus 20: "Honor your father and your mother" (Freedman 2). The obligation of honor must manifest itself in terms of behavior, rather than rely solely on attitude or emotional attachment (Freedman 2). How one honors his or her parents will vary according to the needs and physical conditions of the older generation. Generally, it signifies something as simple as understanding their importance and treating them like the human beings they are (Freedman 3). There are also negative aspects of filial duty in the Jewish tradition. These responsibilities have to do with assisting parents by refraining, at times, from actions that might cause pain and/or shame (Freedman 4), particularly for patients with a terminal illness. People suffering from a terminal illness are at the mercy of a staff who has to care for many patients. Many routines, from being fed to assistance with excretion, create a sense of either incompetence or helplessness, a child-like state. Often, an offspring simply wishes to aid a parent to die with some semblance of dignity (Freedman 6). In this sense, then, "failure to ensure that a parent is spared pain and indignity represents a violation of the prohibitions against striking or cursing a parent" (Freedman 7). This is the violation of Jewish law that occurs when a child neglects responsibility to a parent during the final stages of life.

Judaism emphasizes duties and obligations to community, to God and to parents. The secular contract, on the other hand, focuses on rights. "Within our society, a person is competent if he or she can claim and exercise rights. Within the Jewish perspective, by contrast ... competency is judged relative to duties rather than to rights" (Freedman 9).

Federal Funding for Stem Cell Research

In the past year, federal funding for stem-cell research has become a topic of key concern for research scientists, doctors, patients and theologians. Researchers say that doctors would eventually be able to use stem cells, which are capable of renewing themselves, to replace existing damaged and/or diseased cells. The potential for curing those with Parkinson's and Alzheimer's diseases, diabetes, multiple sclerosis and heart disease, among others, seems enormous, according to many health specialists (Samber "Jewish Groups..." 1).

However, there are problems—not so much of a scientific nature, though these do exist, but more having to do with the intersections of governmental policy, medical ethics and religious concerns. No controversy exists about using adult stem cells in research, because the person requiring medical treatment can generate them. Treatment, theoretically, could be carried out with a patient's own cells (Bohlin 2). Researchers believe, however, that "human ES [embryonic stem cells] cells hold the greatest potential for treatment of degenerative diseases" (Bohlin 2).

The difficulty with using ES cells is that they require the destruction of human embryos. For Roman Catholics and Christian fundamentalists, this is a form of murder. For Jews, who believe life does not begin until approximately 40 days from conception, it is not. Moreover, Jewish ethicists, extrapolating from the rabbinical commentaries, can fall back on the concept of *pikuach nefesh*—that is, the "responsibility to save human life, which overrides almost all other laws." The result is that most Jewish groups, religious and secular, support the idea of using federal funds for stem-cell research.

Distinctions also have been drawn between therapeutic and reproductive research, depending on whether the embryo resides inside or outside the womb. Opponents of ES cell research contend that each frozen embryo stored outside the womb may be perceived as "a unique human being with the full potential to develop into an adult" (Bohlin 3). Regardless how the embryo came to be frozen outside the womb, in their estimation, no end justifies the means of "killing" embryos (Bohlin 3). Jewish philosophers and biomedical ethicists assert, however, that embryos outside the womb are not living beings, and using them in research is "not only permitted, there is a Jewish mandate to do so" (Samber "Jewish Groups..." 1), said Rabbi Elliot Dorff, rector and professor of philosophy at the University of Judaism in Los Angeles. Dorff participated in " Jews & the American Public Square," a Casden Institute forum that was co-sponsored by the Board of Rabbis of Southern California and the Center for Jewish Community Studies/Jerusalem Center for Public Affairs. During the forum, Dorff emphasized that all branches of Judaism have "taken official positions very much in favor of stem-cell research and they (Reform, Conservative and Orthodox Jewry) would see it as a sin" not to explore this possibility for enhancing life.

Initially, most Jewish organizations were silent when the question of federal funding of stem-cell research became part of a national public discussion. The subject of medical experiments revived memories of Hitler's doctors and the sadistic use of humans in research. By association, it seemed a throwback to research in Nazi Germany, when the state made life-and-death decisions without consent and without valuing human life, as described earlier in this chapter. But Jewish groups soon evaluated the proposal on its own terms and "began to voice support for embryonic stem-cell research" (Duskin 44). The emphasis of Jewish law, invariably pragmatic and adaptive, has always been on life on Earth, rather than on some afterlife (Duskin 45). This was reflected last year when the Union of American Hebrew Congregations, the Reform movement's lay organization, sent a letter to President Bush endorsing embryonic stem- cell research. Only God can create life, they wrote the president, "but God has charged human beings with doing everything possible to preserve it" (Duskin 44).

Extending the examination of stem-cell research to human cloning changes the argument substantially and raises additional questions in Jewish law about the parentage of the clone. Some Jewish organizations and ethicists are more tentative here and are staking out a middle ground. The general response has been to differentiate between cloning for medical research (therapeutic cloning) and for reproduction. The Jewish community has endorsed research, but it has backed away from cloning as a form of reproduction (Samber "Cloning…" 1).

Rabbis and Jewish doctors have affirmed that cloning is acceptable under Jewish law. That seems to be a consensus among all branches of Judaism. It is the "dangers of untested biotechnology," along with unanswered questions, which have given them pause (Hirschberg 2). For example: "How will the rules on marriage and incest apply to a clone? Who are a clone's parents? And what does cloning mean for the family structure" (Hirschberg 2)? The scattered questions and answers have led to a tentative consensus: Cloning is permissible, but not yet (Hirschberg 2).

Some Jewish ethicists have adopted a stronger affirmative stand. Mark Pelavin, associate director of the Religious Action Center of Reform Judaism, is concerned that medical advancement might be set back because of a ban on cloning research. Rabbi Michael Broyde, a law professor at Emory University in Atlanta, has written that cloning needs proper supervision, but under those conditions could be perfectly acceptable. He, like others, gives paramount importance to the medical gains (Samber "Cloning..." 2). Also, some rabbis and Jewish experts in medical ethics have pronounced that cloning is not only acceptable, but there may be "an imperative to use it, where it would provide a clear medical benefit—such as solving infertility problems, or creating tissue-matched donors" (Bohlin 3).

However, Dr. Leon R. Kass, President Bush's choice to head the administration's Council on Bio-Ethics, has exercised an influential minority voice. Dr. Kass is Jewish but actively opposes cloning (as does President Bush) and has taken a narrow and limited view of stem-cell research. He has spoken out against congressional legislation that would legalize cloning for research purposes, in large part because he believes cloning is unethical (Kass 1). He fears once a bill that permits cloning for research is passed, it will be impossible to control or prevent the practice to slip over into the reproductive realm. "The only way to effectively ban reproductive cloning is to stop the process from the beginning.... We need to ban all human cloning" (Kass 1). His opinions will help shape American policy in the immediate future.

His passionate opposition is predicated on a number of assumptions: cloning is a form of unethical experimentation on a child-to-be, subjecting a child to enormous developmental risks; it threatens individuality; it "confuses identity by denying the clone two biological parents"; and it is a tremendous step in the wrong direction of eugenics, "turning procreation into manufacture" (Kass 2). Kass assumes that as soon as embryonic clones find their way to the laboratory, "the eugenic revolution will have begun." (Kass 3). He has drawn support from political and intellectual circles. Indeed, despite the religious differences and perspectives, the conflict over stem-cell research and cloning is, at this point, a political one. But framing the debate as political still tends to align Catholics and Christian fundamentalists against Jews and secular humanists.

The late Marlene Marks—a columnist for the Jewish Journal of Los Angeles, a member of the Casden Institute's Advisory Board and an author on Jewish topics—has pointed to a disadvantage faced by the organized, religious Jewish community: American Judaism is faced with the prospect of appearing "to accept the Jewish version of religious truth over" the Christian one. "Our numbers aren't big enough," she wrote (Adler Marks 2). However, secular Judaism has no such disadvantage. The views of its adherents represent the widest kind of diversity on matters of culture, the right to privacy, the separation of church and state and an America " in which all can flourish" (Adler Marks 2).

Diverse groups of Americans have embraced a version of life as it should be lived from the vantage of secular Jews. This includes trivial lifestyle matters such as food, films and comedy, the life shaped by our popular culture and the political causes that find their roots in the Bill of Rights (Adler Marks 2). Marks saw this potential alliance in "America's coarsening political environment" as being ripe for a cause that endorsed using federal funds for stem-cell research, cloning and medical advancement that might benefit all of us (Adler Marks 2).

General Consensus Among Jewish Groups?

The heads of Jewish organizations tend to be cautious and circumspect. At present, despite their support of legislation and continued research, Jewish religious authorities are advising that the research community proceed carefully because "the risk benefit ratio is negative," said Rabbi Moshe David Tendler, a professor of Jewish medical ethics at Yeshiva University. There is the chance that an implanted cloned egg might result in the creation of a monster (Hirschberg 7). Professor Dorff of the

University of Judaism also favors a "go slow" approach, explaining that cloning might pose a risk to the human species (Hirschberg 7). He too favors the continuation of research. Their hesitation is not over the extension of stem cell research; they simply believe that all caution and diligence must be exercised. At present, Dorff favors legislation, as he stated at the April 2002 Casden Institute forum, "Jews & the American Public Square," that "would allow for therapeutic cloning, even though it would not allow for reproductive cloning, and I think that's the exact right line to draw."

In the Reform movement, which endorses cloning, Rabbi Richard Address, director of the movement's Department of Jewish Family Concerns, also has called for "measured, slow research" (Hirschberg 5). His view is echoed by Orthodox Rabbi Pinchas Lipner, dean and founder of the Institute for Jewish Medical Ethics in San Francisco, who advises that we "proceed cautiously and develop moral and ethical guidelines for the research. We must be careful not to create monsters and not to create havoc" (Hirschberg 5). It is the sacredness of human life that underlies their concern, propelling Jewish leaders to endorse the research but urge careful consideration of each step along the way.

Jewish organizations such as Hadassah, the National Council of Jewish Women and the American Jewish Committee also have reached a consensus on the appropriateness and necessity of support for therapeutic stem cell research. The national political division, therefore, has also become religious. Those opposing the research are "the [Roman] Catholic Church, the Southern Baptist Convention and many Christian political action groups— including Focus on the Family, the Family Research Council and the Christian Coalition" (Cooperman 1). They all support a ban on human cloning, including research for medical purposes, as does President George W. Bush.

Meanwhile, Jewish groups have begun to stake out some guidelines and to raise questions, accompanied by cautionary warnings. "Under what circumstances is cloning justified? How far must science advance before it can be tried? And what does it mean to be a clone—carrying DNA that's close to identical to another human being's genetic make-up" (Hirschberg 2)? They are also looking to specific cases that might arise. Will cloning provide a solution for an infertile couple unable to have a child (Hirschberg 6)? Can parents with Tay-Sachs syndrome "avoid the risk of having a doomed child" (Hirschberg 6)?

There are questions about Golems and whether or not a clone is a human being (Hirschberg 10). Also, there are the *halacha* questions. "What if the DNA donor is a non-Jewish woman, but the ovum comes from a Jewish woman who bears the child? Maternity determines Jewishness—but who's the mother?" One suggested answer: "You might need a conversion" (Hirschberg 10).

Along with the questions and the "go slow" warnings, a number of additional issues for further deliberation have been raised by the ethics Advisory Board, "whose members represent a variety of philosophical and theological traditions … in health care ethics" (Zoloth-Dorfman 5). One concern is over control of the fetal or embryo tissue. To whom does consent belong (Zoloth-Dorfman 5)? And perhaps most perplexing of all in political terms, "What is the role of consensus", when we are so "deeply divided over appropriate norms" (Zoloth-Dorfman 5)? The disputes among religious groups, and among secular and religious groups, are so wide-ranging, and the feelings so intense and deep, that consensus may be difficult to achieve. This is especially true given that these are substantive moral disagreements (Zoloth-Dorfman 5).

Meanwhile, science and life barely pause. Several Jewish doctors have begun talking about using cloning techniques as a possible treatment for Alzheimer's and Parkinson's diseases, noting that those particular cells might be capable of being revitalized (Hirschberg 7). Dr. Tendler says that theoretically it should be possible in five years "to make muscle cells that could then be transplanted into the heart to replace damaged tissue" (Hirschberg 8). Without doubt, the political conflict, with its important religious undertones, will continue. Nevertheless, the likelihood of knowledge being suppressed and of scientific breakthroughs halted for an extended period of time seems highly unlikely. The concern for Jews, many of whom are leaders in this ongoing debate, is to make sure that ethical responsibility and respect for human life are consistently upheld. These are principles of Jewish law, but they apply as well to our civic ideals as a nation, and therefore affect all Jews, secular and religious alike.

Conclusion

It is clear that biomedical ethics is highly relevant to our society today, providing insight and direction as we adjust to the latest new medical developments. When we look back with horror on the Nazi regime and on more recent incidents of genocide, the need for a code of biomedical ethics seems all pervasive. It is evident that some of the underlying issues, such as eugenics and euthanasia, lurk beneath the surface of our societal debates today, according to scholars such as Leon Kass. Selective abortion, euthanasia and cloning do echo part of the Darwinian approach to eugenics employed by the Nazis, and to a far lesser extent, by the American government. The survival of the fittest can, perhaps, be seen as the basis for many areas of current medical research, including cloning, selective abortion and stem-cell research. All these issues are based on improving and extending the life of the patient, sometimes at the expense of others. At the same time, stem-cell research and other related developments in medical knowledge do hold the potential for vast improvements in health care and society. Thus, the question posed at the beginning of the chapter resurfaces: How should one ethically respond to these innovations and breakthroughs? They offer incredible hope for our future, but they forshadow the possibility, in the eyes of some critics, of an eventual moral decline.

No easy answers are forthcoming, but like those doctors and philosophers from the 1960s and '70s who took an initial stand on behalf of the rights of patients, biomedical ethicists continue to support the autonomy of the individual. Though many of the specific questions have changed, and have become much more complicated, according to some, the fundamental concern of biomedical ethics remains the same.

Chapter Two

POLITICS:
American Jews and Israel

This chapter closely examines the relationship between American Jews and Israel from the formation of the Jewish state in 1948 to the present. That relationship inevitably was bound by the twin forces of national security and domestic politics, each of which played a determining role in helping to shape United States policy in the Middle East. In the process, American Jews found themselves championing Israel, but also pursuing national and personal issues. Their responses to the new, independent nation often reflected the fact that Jewish Americans lived in a pluralistic society, in which some kept Israel more in the forefront of their political agenda while others were less involved. Only during a period of crisis, such as the Six Day War, have nearly all American Jews strongly recognized their own connection—in terms of history, ethnicity and identity—to Israel.

In the first section, we explore some of the factors that affected the founding of the state of Israel, including the decision by America to support the United Nations' plan for partition; the differences among American Jews and the effect they had on that decision; and the roles Jewish organizations played during that political struggle in the United States. Scholars have pointed out there is no single Jewish American response to Israel, and that only about one third of American Jews consider themselves both strongly attached to and identified with the Jewish state. Indeed, the forces that separate American Jews from Israel, such as language, culture and politics, are at times only overcome by a family's historical and ethnic connections. These bonds become particularly pronounced when Israel comes under siege.

The Six Day War in 1967 serves as a textbook case; it galvanized American Jews of all backgrounds to rally around Israel. The unexpected and rapid victory by Israel against a coalition of Arab forces led to a strong sense of pride and identification. Jews were no longer seen only as victims. It was a lesson that several Jewish organizations—the American Jewish Committee, for one—had to learn along with many American Jews.

The second section covers the dynamics of America's relationship with Israel, from positions of aloofness to solid political alliance. Again, perceptions of national interest and domestic politics held sway through several presidential administrations. Political-party affiliation in the White House seemed not to affect policy decisions. For example, Presidents Reagan and Clinton maintained the closest ties to Israel; Presidents Carter and Eisenhower were the most critical and aloof. We discuss the findings of some scholars who see domestic politics as having the strongest influence on the White House. In their analysis, domestic issues carried over to Congress, especially after changes in campaign laws in the early 1970s that appeared to take place in tandem with the rising influence of American Jews and some of their organizations. Earlier, in the late 1940s, the concerns of the bureaucracy within the State Department had competed with the domestic political agenda. By the 1980s, however, American Jews had become part of the State Department bureaucracy.

Other scholars point to the effect of guilt on the Middle East policy of the United States, particularly under President Truman. America's failure to help Jews during the Nazi reign in Europe was transformed and translated into a humanitarian impulse to right social injustice against Jews, blacks and other minorities.

Finally, we turn to the impact of the September 11 terrorist attacks on the relationship between the United States and Israel and its effects on Jewish Americans. The crisis of September 11 appears to have forged solid bonds between the two nations, each allied in a struggle against terrorism that is parallel and overlapping. One complication has been a surge in anti-Americanism and anti-Israel sentiment among disparate groups in Europe and the Middle East. It is a feeling that has not been confined to Arab and Muslim populations. Its fallout has noticeably affected American Jews. One difference between today and 55 years ago, however, is that Jews in the United States are no longer marginal outsiders. We begin this chapter then, appropriately, with the changes occurring within American society.

Historical Background

Support for Israel by Jewish Americans has always been solid, with differences of opinion typically relegated to debates over how best to provide assistance. The relationship has been complex, fluctuating with the political changes occurring within Israel and, more often, with the alterations in status and the situation of Jews in the United States. To complicate matters, according to Deborah Dash Moore and S. Ilan Troen, "Jews in the United States often projected their own image upon Israeli society, while Israelis fashioned versions of America that spoke to the needs of a new nation struggling to define its values and secure its existence" (Moore and Troen 1-2). Moore, a participant in the *Reappearing American Jew* conference sponsored by the Casden Institute for the Study of the Jewish Role in American Life and Hebrew Union College-Jewish Institute of Religion, and Troen note that American Jews have adapted to a society that celebrates individual achievement, whereas communal participation is prized in Israel (Moore and Troen 3). What binds the two societies, however, is a common heritage, which has led to a sense of shared fate and mutual responsibility (Moore and Troen 2). It is past experiences that link Israelis and American Jews, and these experiences are imbued with a vital sense of currentness in times of crisis, such as the stark nightmare of the Holocaust and the Six Day War.

In the absence of crisis, there is no single, uniform American Jewish response to Israel, although high levels of loyalty and avowed commitment are always present (Seltzer and Cohen 395-414). This finding has generated different responses among scholars. For example, research conducted in May 1948 by the National Opinion Research Center at the University of Chicago found that 90 percent of the Jews in Baltimore approved the establishment of the state of Israel (Geldman 34). That conclusion has consistently been repeated in other surveys. However, in the 1990s, Steven M. Cohen, professor of sociology at Queens College in New York and at Hebrew University in Jerusalem, concluded that American Jewish support for Israel had waned as a function of "increasing alienation from Israel" (Geldman 34). According to Cohen, some Americans are passionate about the Jewish state, some are indifferent and some look for and expect Israel to serve as a Jewish ideal (Cohen 119). Most American Jews, he asserts, have a two-sided involvement with Israel. They claim a deep and passionate commitment, but for two-thirds of those surveyed, their relationship is superficial. Most are pro-Israel in a loose, emotional way but know little about its politics or culture, says Cohen. Few are actually committed Zionists who belong to active Jewish organizations that lobby politically in behalf of the Jewish state; fewer still contemplate ever living in Israel.

Moreover, while most Jewish Americans feel connected to Israel on political grounds, their cultural and spiritual ties are tenuous (Cohen in Gordis and Ben-Horin, 119-135). His overall finding is itself almost a contradiction: Support for Israel is skin deep, except in times of crisis. When a crisis occurs, however, such as the prelude to the Six Day War in 1967 or the Yom Kippur War of 1973, American Jews overwhelmingly rally around the

Jewish nation. They raise money, volunteer personal assistance and, through their Jewish organizations, mount active lobbying campaigns for assistance in Congress and the White House. According to Cohen, it can be said that a commitment to Israel is a central part of American Jewish life and part of the definition of "what it means to be a Jew" (Cohen 122). He adds it also can be said that most American Jews are ignorant of even the most basic aspects of Israeli politics, education and society, and that their involvement with Israel barely affects their private lives or their relationship to Judaism (Cohen 122).

Recent surveys by the American Jewish Committee suggest that the focus of Jews in the United States is decidedly American-centered. Jewish Americans agree life here is preferable to that of life in Israel, and a mere six percent have said they would want their children to live in Israel (Seltzer and Cohen 123). The point reiterated by scholars is that American and Israeli Jews have established two distinctive cultures. They share certain "Jewish concerns and connections," and unite in times of crisis, but they also pursue different paths and visions (Moore and Troen 1). For example, American Jews and Israelis do not share a common language, a national history, or even a common culture. Yiddish, the language of both groups' ancestors, has been mostly lost (Moore and Troen 2). Despite these findings, the general perception among most American Jews is that they "have a sense of kinship with Jews in Israel and a sense of commitment to Israel's well-being and survival" (Ginsberg 21).

Professor Benjamin Ginsberg, director of the Center for the Study of American Government at Johns Hopkins University, says the three most important bonds that link the two nations are tradition, identity and military power (Ginsberg 21). The shared traditions pre-date the establishment of national boundaries, because they are religious as well as ethnic. They surface on Jewish holidays and tie Jews to one another during ceremonies such as funerals, weddings and bar and bat mitzvahs. These life passages become recognizable symbols for all Jews, irrespective of national boundary lines. Identity formation plays a more circumspect role. American Jews are silent on the issue in front of non-Jews, but among each other will acknowledge a fear that perhaps one day Jews might be forced to leave the United States. Israel is the insurance policy for Jews in America, if there ever is a violent breakout of anti-Semitism (Ginsberg 22).

Finally, Ginsberg says that American support for Israel is also based in part on Israel's military success. American Jews despised the image of the Jew as coward, victim and physical weakling. In 1967, when Israel's air and defense forces defeated the combined Arab armies of Egypt, Syria and Jordan in six days, American Jews were jubilant and Jewish institutions discovered that Israel became a central focus, especially as an "effective rallying point for their fund-raising and membership activities" (Ginsberg 23).

Ardie Geldman, executive director of AMIT Women's Organization in Efrat, Israel, says the enthusiasm of Jewish Americans for Israel after the Six Day War should not be viewed as a commitment to Zionism, at least in the classic European meaning of establishing a homeland for Jews in Palestine. For most American Jews, Zionism equals "supporting the right of the state of Israel to exist as a Jewish state in peace and security" (Geldman 33). In that way, nearly all Americans could be considered Zionists. Later, cynics would define an American Zionist as being "one Jew who collects money from a second Jew to make it possible for a third Jew to live in Israel" (Geldman 33).

Becoming American Jews

Throughout the 1950s, American Jews were only marginally committed to the state of Israel, although they were pleased the United Nations and the United States had approved the partition plan that created the state of Israel (Auerbach 21). The crises of partition and the fight with the Arabs in 1948 were considered part of history.

Instead, the task that preoccupied Jewish Americans after World War II was to find ways to engage in and become accepted by American society. "The major drive of Jews in the United States during this period," said professor Yossi Shain of Georgetown University, "was toward developing an integrated identity.... Although American Jews were enthusiastic about the birth of Israel as an asylum for displaced Jews, Zionism and Israel's perception of the Diaspora were less significant 'to their own personal identity' " (Shain 167). Shain lectured at USC on "New Thinking About Diasporas in International Affairs," focusing on Diasporas in conflict resolution, their role in the world economy and the transmission of values across frontiers. The presentation was co-sponsored by the Jesse M. Unruh Institute of Politics, the Center for International Studies and the Casden Institute for the Study of the Jewish Role in American Life.

The fear among American Jews was that Jewish nationalism, whether it meant unassimilated immigrants in the United States or a strident call from Israel for the backing of Jews worldwide, might increase suspicion in the United States of dual loyalty (Shain 176). After the recognition of Israel in 1948, for example, several American Jewish leaders took a combative stance toward David Ben Gurion, Israel's first prime minister. Ben Gurion assumed that Jews worldwide would flock to the new Jewish state. All Jews needed to make Israel their home, he asserted (Ginsburg 22). American Jewish leaders disagreed. The head of the American Zionist movement, Abba Hillel Silver, insisted that because Jews had a very special relationship to Israel, they also had a right to wield political influence over Israeli policies. Given that the majority of Jews now lived in the United States, Silver intimated that Jewish organizations here were part of Israel's constituency and had a right to affect policy. It was at that point that the Israeli prime minister issued his famous dictum: Jews sitting in Cleveland had no say over policies that originated in Tel Aviv (Ginsburg 22). If Silver wanted a political voice in the new Jewish nation, all he had to do was move to Israel and become part of the political process. Eventually, by the early 1950s, an agreement was reached. Ben Gurion agreed to stop declaring Israel was the only true home for Jews, and American Jewish leaders would in turn lend their voices to gain financial aid and political backing in Washington for Israel while refraining from interfering in Israeli politics. American Jews were morally committed to Israel, but under no obligation to live there (Ginsburg 23).

Some Jewish organizations were initially less than enthusiastic about an independent Israel. The American Jewish Committee, for example, was dominated by Jewish leaders who were not favorably inclined toward the creation of a new Jewish state (Grossman, L. 29-31). Jerome A. Chanes, associate director of the National Foundation for Jewish Culture, has written about the committee and its attitude toward Israel in a chapter devoted to Jewish advocacy and Jewish interest groups in *Jews in American Politics*, edited by L. Sandy Maisel and Ira N. Forman. He notes that the committee was established in 1906 by a small core of German Jews with a very specific purpose: to mobilize Jews in America to combat the sweep of anti-Semitism. It was a small, self-selected, elitist group that served as a highly effective voice for American Jews on policy issues. It was thoughtful and deliberative and dealt with issues related to ethnicity, pluralism, human rights and inter-religious affairs (Maisel and Forman 104). Its form and structure dovetailed with American life and institutions. One of its chief concerns was to avoid suggesting there was another nation American Jews might prefer, thereby presumably antagonizing the American majority (Chanes in Maisel and Forman 104).

Lawrence Grossman, a staff member of the American Jewish Committee, took a sabbatical from the organization to research its records and complete an essay about its early history, specifically about its transformation during the Six Day War crisis. The committee, he says, was officially not a Zionist organization (Grossman, L. 28) and while it endorsed the partition of Palestine in 1947-48, it did so somewhat reluctantly. Its leadership wanted to avoid the perception that American Jews could be anything but 100 percent American. They also wished to protect their own "territory." Jewish organizations in the United States functioned as the primary institutions representing the interests of American Jews. They were regarded by their leaders as something akin to the "Jewish state" in America (Ginsburg 22). The formation of Israel, an actual homeland for Jews, was seen as a competitive threat to the AJC's role, somewhat like the danger that the "return of Christ represented to Dostoyevsky's Grand Inquisitor" (Grossman, L. 22). In later years, two AJC presidents, Irving

Engel and Morris Abram, acknowledged the difficulty they had in adjusting to a Jewish nation in the Middle East. Engel "was opposed to the creation of a new state for the Jews." Abram, who became president of the AJC in 1964, recalled being avowedly anti-Zionist while he was growing up in Georgia (Grossman, L. 36). Just before the outbreak of the Six Day War in 1967, a question was raised at an annual AJC meeting: "What would the American administration think when Jews, so many of whom vocally opposed the Vietnam War, asked for American intervention in the Middle East" (Grossman, L. 44)?

Mass meetings in Jewish communities around the country, national rallies and public demonstrations suggested that the Jewish American public was very much concerned about the fate of Israel in 1967. Abram, the then-president of the AJC, softened his stance and began to lean toward assisting Israel when war broke out. The first news reports came from Arab media outlets and reported an Israeli debacle. It was enough to frighten many American Jews. That day, Abram wrote, "marks the beginning of the revival of a frightful collective unconscious in world Jewry" (Grossman, L. 46). When despair was at its peak, Engel received two successive telephone calls. The first was from the Israeli ambassador in Washington saying that American intervention was not necessary: Israel had already won the war. The second was from Joseph Califano, special assistant to President Johnson, who said, "Israel has won the greatest victory in the shortest campaign in all history" (Grossman, L. 48).

The anxiety over the war, followed by Israel's "greatest victory," produced a radical about-face on the part of the AJC and its leaders. This was not only because its rank and file had demonstrated an intense identification with Israel in a time of crisis, but also because the leaders themselves had recognized their own connections to Jews in Israel. Abram's changed attitude was reflected in his statement that American Jews "hold one thing in common with Jews everywhere in the world, and that is a peculiar vulnerability. . . . Jews do live on a precipice" (Grossman, L. 50). At the AJC annual meeting in 1968, a resolution was passed that put the AJC on record as having a "personal attachment and profound sense of a shared history and destiny that organically connect American Jews to Israel" (Grossman, L. 53).

The Turning Point

It took Israel's success in the Six Day War for most American Jews and their organizations to embrace Israel passionately. One political scientist noted, "American Jews were better known for their opposition to Vietnam than for any policy toward Israel" (Maisel and Forman 259). Indeed, Jewish involvement and influence was peripheral at best. The military victory served as a tremendous jolt, engendering pride and a sense of identification. Commentators have written that the Six Day War was a "transformational event in Jewish American history" (Zeitz 1). Elie Wiesel, a writer, Holocaust survivor and Nobel Peace Prize winner, noted in 1968: "I would go even further and say that the change was total, for it involved my very being as both a person and as a Jew" (Zeitz 1).

Many American Jews were surprised by their personal response; they had not realized how deeply connected they felt to Israel. Shortly before the war was launched, Egypt, Syria and Jordan encircled Israel. Emergency fund-raising sessions were called in the United States (Zeitz 3). Young American Jews, who had been called apathetic and disinterested in Israel, signed up to fill in spots on kibbutzim and in factories that were emptied of workers because of the military mobilization. By summer's end, more than 10,000 American Jewish students had volunteered and traveled to Israel (Zeitz 3). "Once Israeli soldiers heroically defended their homeland, Zionism became—and for exactly a decade remained—the new religion of American Jews" (Auerbach 21).

In several cities, American Jewish organizations began to promote trips to and raise funds for Israel from Jews. After the Six Day War, Israel "became the central focus of American Jewish life" (Ginsburg 23). Community fund drives in America were built around supporting Israel. As Jews in America were becoming more secular, Israel began to serve as the rallying point for American Jewish organizations. It turned into a source of fund-raising, membership recruitment, and, eventually, the impetus to strengthen what was seen as a weakening sense of Jewish identity.

Further Changes

In 1977, Menachem Begin was elected prime minister of Israel. The government of Israel was now seen as conservative, religious and militarily assertive. Auerbach writes that Begin's "fusion of Jewish nationalism and religious Orthodoxy contradicted the secular universalist tenets of modern liberalism" that typified mainstream American Judaism (Auerbach 21). Jewish leaders in the United States affirmed their support for the new Israeli government, but feelings of uneasiness among some remained. Jewish American liberals such as Rabbi Arthur Hertzberg of New Jersey and journalist I. F. Stone in Washington became critical of the Jewish state, arguing that Israel needed to follow a moral course that conformed to America's highest ideals (Auerbach 22).

With the emergence of the *intifada*, the uprising in the streets of the West Bank driven initially by Palestinian teenagers hurling rocks at military personnel in 1987, Israel came under increased criticism for "its brutal military occupation and suppression of Palestinian national rights" (Auerbach 22). Orthodox rabbis and right-wing settlers appeared to be shaping Israeli policy regarding the increased settlements on the West Bank, and American Jews believed they were now forced to choose, not between Israel and America but "between Israel and liberalism" (Auerbach 22). Yitzhak Rabin's election as Israeli prime minister in 1992 appeared to appease American liberals, and the 1993 peace accords suggested Israel was back on the "correct" path, as far as Jewish American liberals were concerned. However, according to Auerbach, Rabin's support in the United States came from Jews who "were least knowledgeable about Judaism, least religiously observant, least likely to visit Israel, [and] most tolerant of intermarriage" (Auerbach 23).

Jews in America were still split between those who supported the Israeli government, regardless who was in office, and those who opposed settlements and a hard line with the Palestinians. The case involving Jonathan Pollard, an American Jew in the Defense Department caught spying for Israel in November 1985, intensified the split. The spying incident looked like a conflict between the interests of the United States and those of the Jewish state. The consensus was that, "if forced to choose between American interests and Israel's interests, most American Jews would choose the former" (Geldman 37).

Current Commitment, Current Reservations

Jack Wertheimer, provost and professor of American Jewish history at the Jewish Theological Seminary of America in New York and a participant in the Casden Institute and HUC-JIR *Reappearing American Jew* conference, writes that AJC surveys show Jewish identification with Israel declining in the United States from 1993 to 1997 (Wertheimer 3). In the 1997 study, American Jews over 60 years old reported the closest ties to Israel and those under 40 appeared to feel most distant (Wertheimer 3). At that time, the weakening bonds of the younger generations were attributed to battles over religious pluralism in the Jewish state. For instance, according to Israeli law (heavily influenced by the Orthodox population in Jerusalem), only Orthodox rabbis can officiate at conversions. A Jew might still be a citizen of Israel, but without an official conversion he or she cannot marry or be buried there. This law offended many American Jews, particularly rabbis, who saw this as making the Reform and Conservative denominations of Judaism non-legitimate (Brackman 1-3). Each branch has a small following in Israel, but Reform and Conservative Judaism look to many native-born Israelis like offshoots of American life, rather than of the Jewish religion, and as such foreign to Israel. The ensuing conflict has been viewed in Israel as largely exacerbated by the American rabbinate's use of the pulpit to raise the saliency of the issue, which in turn has offended and alienated many American Jews (Brackman 9).

Wertheimer has a different perception of recent causes and effects. He believes that the disengagement of various sectors of American Jewry from Israel is actually part of "a growing indifference here to all things Jewish, and especially to an identification with the Jewish people" (Wertheimer 3). He sees the individual issues—Pollard's spying; the absence of religious pluralism in Israel; 200,000 Jews living on the West Bank; and the rise of the Likud Party in Israel—as rationalizations used to justify the disenchantment with Israel on the part of some American Jews (Wertheimer 4).

Wertheimer believes that American Jews who have distanced themselves from Israel are actually removing themselves from a Jewish identity in the United States and are now primarily engaged in the wider American society, where religion and ethnicity are perceived as distractions. That is not the whole story, he adds. A core group of American Jews still identifies strongly with Israel and with their own sense of Jewishness. Despite a number of Jews in the United States who are alienated, there are many others who hold fast to a strong affiliation with Israel and a Jewish life (Wertheimer 6).

While these alternative paths reinforce American pluralism, they threaten to make hollow the slogan of American Jewish organizations that "we are one" (Wertheimer 4). We are at least two Jewish communities and probably many more, with the one proviso that "in moments of adversity ... cultural disparities have been bridged. ... In crisis and war, American Jews have repeatedly rallied to the banner of philanthropic Zionism, offering financial support and lobbying muscle" (Wertheimer 4). That "lobbying muscle" continues to be evident in places where there are significant numbers of Jews, including New York, Miami, Chicago and Los Angeles.

The importance of a "Jewish vote" and Jewish preferences was evident in New York City in 1999. Ehud Barak, then prime minister of Israel, spoke warmly of President and Mrs. Clinton's concerns for the peace process in Israel. Hillary Clinton was then campaigning for the U.S. Senate seat in New York State. Republican New York Mayor Rudolph Giuliani, who had been considering a Senate run, interpreted this as an endorsement by Barak of Clinton's candidacy. Giuliani asked Jerusalem Mayor Ehud Olmert, a friend and Likud Party member, to speak on his behalf during a fund-raiser in the United States. "Although neither Israeli ... actually endorsed either Senate candidate, their involvement underscores the importance that both Clinton and Giuliani place[d] on their relationships with Israel," and on the impact such recognition had on the behavior of Jewish voters (Lambert 1-3).

America's Role in the Middle East

The response of Jewish American voters to Israel often turns foreign policy into a domestic political issue. A nation's foreign policy generally is determined by two separate but related factors: national security interests and domestic politics. It is largely in this context that the foreign policy of the United States in the Middle East has been examined.

At the end of World War II, American Jewish insecurities—about anti-Semitism, discrimination in education and the workplace, and the perception of being considered outsiders in Christian America—were still in place. These insecurities were accompanied by the divisions and factions that had helped make Jews, in UCLA professor Steven Spiegel's term, so "ineffective" during the 1930s. (Spiegel 230). Jews were still supplicants. Their voice in American party politics was slight and Jewish influence in foreign affairs was therefore quite negligible, often characterized by failure and tragedy. They were still seen by American government officials and members of Congress, in the early days of the Cold War, as left-leaning liberals and displaced persons without much power (Spiegel 252-257).

This was the mind-set in the spring of 1948 when partition and the creation of Israel came before the United Nations. The likelihood that Jewish support could persuade the Truman administration to back partition and the formation of a new Jewish state appeared slim. Not only were American Jews seen as marginal, but the State Department bureaucracy believed American security interests rested with the oil producers in the Arab nations, not with David Ben Gurion and his fellow Zionists looking to start a Jewish homeland (Lewis 366).

Several unexpected factors came into play. First and foremost was guilt: guilt in the aftermath of German persecution of the Jews, which the United States had ignored, and guilt that helped develop among all Americans a "humanitarian impulse to deal with resettling the homeless, the refugees and the victims of Hitler's Europe" (Lewis 365). The "humanitarian impulse" was reinforced by the exigencies of domestic politics. While the United Nations was scheduled to vote on the founding of Israel in May 1948, an American presidential election would take place in November of that year. The Democratic incumbent, President Harry S. Truman, was heading into a tight race in which he appeared to be the underdog. Truman adviser Clark Clifford saw Jewish contributors and voters—especially in such key states as New York, Illinois, Ohio and California—as vital for the Democratic Party (Mart 195).

For a brief period, President Truman vacillated, at one point deciding that he could not support Israel, in part because of recommendations from the State Department and in part because the notion of a Jewish nation seemed too particularistic and theocratic (Wertheimer 3). When he saw that Zionist fighters in Palestine had held their own during fighting in April and early May of 1948, he was reassured that Israel could survive (Spiegel 258). Another Holocaust, this time in the Middle East, would be unacceptable and was not something an American president wanted to face for moral and political reasons. In the end, President Truman parted with his State Department advisers, justifying his decision on nationalistic grounds: He feared the Russians might be the first to recognize the new Jewish state. Eventually, President Truman's decision to endorse Israel was based on a mix of humanitarian concerns and recognition that Jewish support might be essential to his chances for reelection (Spiegel 258). He managed to appease the opponents in the State Department by embargoing arms to the Jewish community in Palestine. The United States had voted for Israel in the crucial UN vote, but there was nothing special about the relationship set in place, at least on the part of the American government.

Dynamic Changes

Two events eventually altered the 1948 political reality. First, Jews became a significant force in American domestic politics beginning in the late 1960s. Second, the increasing prominence and power of Israel in the Middle East, particularly after the victory in the Six Day War, led to a sense within the United States administration that its interests and those of Israel were joined (Spiegel 252). It was only years later—during Nixon's presidency in 1970, when the Palestinian Liberation Organization and Syria challenged King Hussein of Jordan in the crisis known as Black September—that the special strategic relationship between Israel and the United States, and the need to protect American interests in the region, clearly emerged. During Israel's first 20 years, the "special relationship" between the two nations could hardly be said to exist (Lewis 365).

Professor Michelle Mart of Penn State takes a different tack. She believes that while oil and domestic politics may have been competing political factors in the struggle to create Israel, "the vital ingredient in American support for the Jewish state was the triumph of a humanitarian ideal that redefined political considerations as a universalist concern" (Mart 182). Her view is that recognition and support of Israel were a direct response to the suffering of Holocaust survivors, and that President Truman sought to achieve some form of justice for the European refugees and the American Jews who had experienced anti-Semitism (Mart 182). All Americans in 1948 were ennobled, according to Mart, by a "commitment to humanitarianism, morality and political justice," and those values were at the forefront of the conflict over the birth of Israel (Mart 183). The key value was that of decency triumphing over racism and anti-Semitism, underscored by the notion of a melting pot that minimized ethnicity and particularity in favor of assimilation and universality.

It was President Truman's evolution as a politician, reflecting "the changing standards of acceptability in postwar public culture," that helped shape his commitment to civil rights and the melting pot, according to professor Mart. It also led him angrily to reject anti-Semitism (Mart 189). One problem for President Truman and Jewish Zionists was that their opponents criticized the particularism of a Jewish state, which seemed to defy the foundations of this new humanitarianism. The struggle between

Truman and his State Department on this issue became a national debate. Thirty-three state legislatures, 40 governors and about half of Congress pressed the president to support Israel. Meanwhile, opposition leaders pointed to British objections, and violence between Arabs and Jews in the Middle East; they argued that the creation of a Jewish state would be a denial of universalism and a rejection of the melting pot ideal (Mart 190-192). Behind the scenes, President Truman's special assistant, Clark Clifford, played an important part in persuading the Democratic president to endorse partition. Clifford's role was to help reelect the president in 1948, and it seemed to many observers that in addition to his avowed humanitarianism, Clifford's reasons were definitely political (Mart 194).

Nevertheless, foreign policy interests dominated American decisions in the Middle East from 1948 to 1967. The Cold War with the Russians eclipsed most other concerns, and Israel was not a major consideration for a succession of American presidents, regardless of political party affiliation. For example, even though President Truman had backed the creation of the state in 1948 (Spiegel 260), his national security advisers were united in their concern to secure Arab cooperation in maintaining oil supplies for Europe. With such delicate negotiations playing out internationally, Israel was simply a burden the United States could barely afford (Spiegel 260).

Truman's successor, President Eisenhower, was even more emphatic. John Foster Dulles, his Secretary of State, was determined to push for a Baghdad Pact—something akin to a Near East NATO—in a further effort to contain the then Soviet Union. When Israel joined the British and the French in invading Egypt and the Suez Canal in 1956, Eisenhower was furious. He forced all three nations to retreat from the invasion. Oil and the Cold War were the central foreign policy concerns of the United States, and Israel's action in the Suez Canal appeared to jeopardize our relations with the Arab nations.

The perception of America burdened by its support of Israel carried through the Kennedy and Johnson administrations in the 1960s. The pressing domestic issues of the civil rights movement and American involvement in the Vietnam War overwhelmed President Johnson's tenure. With the start of the Six Day War in 1967, international politics, specifically the Middle East's instability, made its way onto an already crowded American agenda. The region became an important chip in the international confrontations with the Russians. For American Jews, the Six Day War caused a surge in ethnic identification, and many began to shift some of their civil rights involvement to Israel. Most still backed the Democrats, but a number of middle- and upper-middle-class Jews became Republicans. No longer taken for granted by the Democrats, Jews found themselves courted by both parties (Spiegel 261).

After the Six Day War in 1967, there was little doubt in the mind of subsequent United States presidents that the Middle East was of paramount importance to American foreign policy interests. Arab oil was essential for the economies of the United States and Western Europe, and the battle for control of the region's oil made the area a critical one in the Cold War conflict with the Soviet Union. The political struggle to allow nearly 1,000,000 Soviet Jews to emigrate to Israel also linked the Jewish state to America in the struggle with the communist bloc. Israel's military strength demonstrated in the Six Day War , combined with its democratic institutions, made it a likely ally for the United States. It was the one nation in the region that Christian and Jewish Americans could identify with, partly for religious reasons and partly because the core immigrant base in Israel and the United States had immigrated from Europe (Moore and Troen 4).

The recognition that the United States had major foreign policy interests in the Middle East coincided with the rise in influence of American Jews. With anti-Semitism on the decline, Jews found themselves no longer barred from access to leading institutions of education, medicine, law, media and government. They became heads of universities and law schools, took prominent positions in government, including the State Department and congressional committees, and held key positions at national newspapers such as *The New York Times* and national magazines such as *Time* and *The New Republic*. Jews also became major contributors to political candidates of both parties. All of this was accompanied by the rise in importance of Jewish organizations and lobby groups. The American Israel Public Affairs Committee, one of the most powerful and effective lobbying groups in Washington, became a high-profile agency in advocacy positions championing Israel's interests (Maisel and Forman 111). Jewish organizations such as the Anti-Defamation League, the American Jewish Committee and the Conference of Presidents expanded their foreign policy activities. By the time President Clinton took office, it was customary for American presidents to consult with leaders of Jewish organizations whenever Middle East issues affecting Israel were on the table.

Not that all presidents after Lyndon Johnson were as favorable to Israel or to the notion that Israeli and American interests were identical. For example, some commentators have singled out Jimmy Carter as departing from those views. His intention was to improve relations with the Arab nations, believing that if he could bring a settlement to the region that satisfied them, he could resolve the energy crisis and reduce tensions with Russia and Third World countries. President Reagan seemed to Jewish groups to put the emphasis back on Israel as the center of American policy in the Middle East. However, his successor, President Bush, adopted a hard line on guaranteeing loan agreements to Israel as long as its Likud Party prime ministers continued to advance the interests and numbers of settlers on the West Bank. President Clinton reversed matters in turn, forming strong alliances with Labor prime ministers Rabin and Barak. He then attempted to bolster American interests and his own personal reputation with the achievement of a peace agreement in the Middle East (Lewis 364-378). These changes in approach suggest that the party affiliation of the United States president has had little effect on policies toward Israel.

The Domestic Front

American Jewish lobby groups did not concentrate all their efforts on the White House. After the Watergate scandal in the mid-1970s and efforts at reform, political action committees (PACs) came into their own. They provided a way for Jewish organizations to raise and funnel money into campaigns supporting candidates sympathetic to Israel, or conversely, to oppose candidates viewed as hostile to Israel (Maisel and Forman 111). This proved highly successful, although adopting a single-issue cause of support for Israel led to fissures in the broad American Jewish community. Liberal Jews disapproved of conservative politicians whose voting record on civil rights, education and labor reform went against what were perceived as Jewish domestic interests. Divisions within the American Jewish community increased, as support for Israel was seen as the overriding issue. Meanwhile, Israel gained strong backing in the United States Congress. Several lawmakers gathered key Jewish staff members to help formulate legislation and provide a counterweight to policies made in the White House. Few were more important to Jewish interests than Henry Jackson, a Democratic senator from Washington. Jackson was not Jewish, but had a staff of knowledgeable, aggressive Jewish assistants. He helped pass the Jackson-Vanik Amendment in 1974, which tied favored nation trade status for the then Soviet Union to a policy of permitting Soviet Jews to leave the country freely. He also championed Israeli interests among congressional Democrats. His "anti-communist, pro-Israeli positions legitimized Jewish analysts who offered alternative policy perspectives to those espoused by the State Department" (Spiegel 262-263).

Beyond 2000

Within the past decade, Jewish lobbying groups in America have become a formidable presence. Their voices are heard on matters affecting all regions of the Middle East. Although members of Congress have grown skeptical of foreign aid, Jewish groups have helped persuade a Republican dominated Congress to pass additional funds to aid Palestinians in 1995 and 1998. In 1994, American Jews lobbied for financial assistance for Jordan, after it concluded a treaty with Israel. By the turn of the century, American Jewish groups had become major players in the coalition that was uniting around "a global and internationalist perspective on foreign policy" (Spiegel 265).

Despite the gains, scholars such as Jack Wertheimer believe the strong political position held by Jews could change overnight. A new president whose perception of United States foreign policy needs clashed with Israel—such as President Carter, who sought to deal first with Arab needs, or the current President Bush, who opposed Israel's settlements on the West Bank—could curtail foreign aid and restrict access to military equipment.

On the domestic front, divisions among American Jews over Israel have grown wider in the past decade. The Labor-Likud conflict has developed its American counterpart with a reinvigorated Zionist Organization of America under the leadership of Morton Klein attacking the Oslo peace proposals, while Americans for Peace Now and the New Israel Fund champion them. AIPAC and many other Jewish organizations have rallied behind the policies of successive Israeli governments, but at the same time authors for *Tikkun* magazine and some Jewish scholars on the left have been more critical or have put forward alternative policy options (see Wertheimer 5). Disputes among American Jews may breathe life into the community and create more active and dynamic public involvement, instead of leaving decisions in the hands of a small cadre of Jewish leaders and organizations, but they also reduce the political effectiveness of Jews as a perceived united influence group.

The bottom line is that American Jews currently enjoy considerable influence in the formulation of foreign policy in the Middle East. They are a special interest group in American society and have become quite successful after 60 years (1910-70) of functioning on the sidelines. But if American foreign policy perspectives change, and/or if the role of Jews in domestic politics is either diminished or fractured as Jews merge into the American mainstream, all that may be altered.

Jewish Americans After September 11: Ties That Bind[1]

Relations between Israel and the United States have fluctuated between highs and lows these past 54 years, pivoting on

---

[1] Scholarly articles and studies are not available on this topic and probably will not be published for at least another year or two. Hence, for this section, we must rely on commentaries and articles that have appeared in popular magazines and journals.

perceptions of American national security interests and the urgent pragmatism of domestic politics. In times of crisis for Israel, American Jews have responded with overwhelming support, and usually the United States has backed the Jewish state.

This appears to be the pattern that had evolved at the time of the September 11 attacks on New York and the Pentagon, along with the forced crash in Pennsylvania of another passenger plane seized by terrorists. However, there is one significant difference: The crisis this time is one experienced first-hand by the United States, with a separate though related critical situation continuing in Israel. The two nations have been joined, albeit involuntarily, and the Bush administration's support for Israel has become more deeply entrenched. Yoram Hazony, Israeli author of the book *The Jewish State: The Struggle for Israel's Soul*, former adviser to ex-Israeli Prime Minister Benjamin Netanyahu and director of the Shalom Center, an institute for social thought and policy in Jerusalem, wrote, "In the wake of the terror attacks, the strategic interests of Israel and the United States have been brought into greater convergence than at any time since the end of the Cold War. At the same time, these interests have been translated into moral terms, putting the two countries clearly on the same side of a larger conflict" (Hazony 15).

Political support for Israel in the United States has not been confined to the White House. Members of Congress from both major parties have been outspoken in their declarations. They have commented on the threats faced by Israel from terrorists and have observed that these perils link the two nations, which have a mutual interest in combating modern-day terrorism. In November 2001, "89 members of the Senate sent a letter to President Bush urging the administration to stop pressuring Israel in its conflict with the Palestinians" (Hazony 18). The message was spelled out more than once by a number of congressmen: The two nations were fighting the same war; the tactics employed by the enemy were the same; and the United States needed to stand solidly with its ally, Israel.

These sentiments were echoed in newspaper and magazine columns by such prominent Jewish and non-Jewish Americans as Harvard law professor Alan Dershowitz, former United Nations Ambassador Jeane Kirkpatrick, former Secretary of Education William J. Bennett, columnists Charles Krauthammer of *The New Republic* and William Safire of *The New York Times* and *Weekly Standard* publisher William Kristol (Hazony 19). Their columns served as reflections of public opinion in the United States, confirmed by a Gallup Poll, a CBS News/*New York Times* Poll and one conducted for NBC News and *The Wall Street Journal* in November 2001. *Newsweek* columnist George Will summed up the perception: "Tuesday morning (September 11), Americans were drawn into the world that Israelis live in every day'" (Hazony 21).

While President Bush, Congress and leading journalists felt this way, not all Americans and most definitely not all Europeans shared this view. A number of European journalists, intellectuals and students were quick to associate the attacks on the World Trade Center in New York and the Pentagon with American support for Israel in the Middle East. One writer noted that the BBC in Great Britain kept repeating in its news broadcasts that "the only reason [Muslims] hate the United States and the only reason the United States was targeted by terrorists is because the United States has 'failed to end Israeli occupation of Palestinians' " (Plaut 1).

This view appeared to have great currency among Arab and Muslim journalists and within the governments that often control the Arab press. In November 2001, Abraham H. Foxman, director of the Anti-Defamation League, wrote an op-ed piece in the *New York Daily News* saying that a Taliban security chief in Afghanistan had told four American journalists that more than 4,000 World Trade Center workers had been advised to take September 11 off. The security chief claimed the attack had been planned by the Mossad, Israel's intelligence arm, as a way of creating a backlash in the United States against the Arab nation. Alternatively, it was explained that information had been leaked by a reliable American source, the CIA. These accounts, according to Foxman, were published as authoritative reports in Syria, Pakistan and Iran (Foxman 1). It was the dominant message, anti-Israel and anti-American, that was passed along to the Arab masses and at times found its way without skepticism to Muslim readers in the United States.

A story in London's *Daily Telegraph* written by Petronella Wyatt, a non-Jewish British journalist, observed that opposition to Israel had increased since the September 11 terrorist attacks in the United States and had apparently metamorphosed into anti-Semitism. It was now acceptable to vent anti-Semitic feelings at "respectable London dinner tables," the British journalist wrote (Grossman, R. 1). One example included an expletive casually hurled at Israel by the French ambassador to Great Britain at a party.

Israeli writer and translator Hillel Halkin, writing in *Commentary* in February 2002, believes that the eagerness with which these sentiments have been embraced is a reflection not just of anti-Israel feelings but of anti-Semitism as well. His evidence is anecdotal, but overwhelming in its detail: Jewish friends in France and Spain encountering open hostility; a story in *Le Nouvel Observateur*, a well-respected French weekly magazine of the left, reporting as fact that Israeli soldiers rape Palestinian women as a matter of policy, so that families will slaughter them as a way of redeeming honor; and a separate article in London's daily *Evening Standard* concluding that Israel did not deserve to exist any longer. In a column by the publisher of the German weekly *Der Spiegel* as well as in the *International Herald Tribune*, denouncements of Israel are common.

All of this is accompanied by anti-Semitic incidents in Western Europe (Halkin 2). For Halkin, the "anti-Semitism has grown in direct proportion to Palestinian violence against Israel." The two are and always have been intertwined , he says (Halkin 8). Since the Holocaust, the anti-Semitism has been suppressed, or at least not voiced often. It has taken the form of anti-Zionism and has been expressed as opposition to Israel and its treatment of Palestinians in Israel and in the West Bank and Gaza. But, Halkin states, "the new anti-Israelism is nothing but the old anti-Semitism in disguise" (Halkin 8). What makes it worrisome for him is that support for Israel is difficult to obtain and justify simply on the grounds of protecting the national interests of other countries. Israel ultimately requires broad public backing for its existence in its own right. Yet up to this point Israel has relied on the steadily generous backing of individual American Jews and the United States Congress, as well as humanitarian support. In the wake of September 11, Halkin says that because of this backing, there is an additional risk for Jews and all Americans. "The undermining of Israel is anti-Semitism's primary goal" (Halkin 9).

Some American universities have been the scene of such anti-Semitic incidents. At San Francisco State University, a group of Jewish students was escorted to safety by police after staging a peace rally. Some of the crowd reportedly screamed in rage: "Get out or we will kill you!" and "Hitler didn't finish the job!" (Nordlinger 2). At Harvard University, professor Ruth Wisse, a celebrated scholar of Yiddish, has complained that "Malice toward Israel and those who support it is now acceptable among people who might have felt the same way before, but took pains not to make it visible" (Nordlinger 3). She added that Jewish students on campus have become rattled and are not quite sure how to respond (Nordlinger 3).

Several Jewish students have turned for assistance to the campus Republicans. At Harvard, the Republican Club held its annual dinner at the university's Hillel; at the University of Michigan, it was the College Republicans and the conservative Young Americans for Freedom who demonstrated their support for Israel, alongside the campus Hillel group, after a conference sponsored by a number of University of Michigan departments and the Office of Multi-Ethnic Student Affairs purportedly included anti-Semitic content (Nordlinger 4). One response from the larger Jewish community has been to try to aid Jewish students by providing information and background on the Middle East through the campus Hillel organizations, which have also tried to organize programs to bring more Jewish students to Israel.

The extent of anti-Semitism on campus has been a source of continuing debate. In response to those who contend that it became a great threat in 2001-02, professor David Myers, vice chair of the history department at UCLA and a prominent Jewish studies scholar, argued in the *Jewish Journal of Greater Los Angeles* (Oct. 18, 2002): "There is cause for vigilance on campuses, as a small number of faculty and students use the pretext of criticism of Israel to advance an anti-Semitic agenda. But the key point to bear in mind is proportion. The number of voices tinged with hatred of Jews is small, I suspect, compared to the amount of anti-Muslim or anti-Arab sentiment on campus and beyond. More importantly, those few voices do not herald an anti-Semitic tidal wave. As recently as June 2002, the Anti-Defamation League, whose job is to fight anti-Semitism, concluded that 'campus faculty and students are the least anti-Semitic among Americans' and that 'anti-Semitism on United States college campuses is virtually nonexistent.' "

More broadly within American society, the reaction against Israel has been fairly muted since September 11. A poll by the Pew Research Center for the People and the Press in December 2001 showed that 35 percent of Americans believed that "the United States has been too supportive of Israel." Forty-five percent of the American respondents thought the opposite (Halkin 9). But the Internet has been filled with denunciations of Israel and American Jews (Grossman, R. 1).

For their part, American Jews have responded to the September 11 attacks like most other Americans: with sadness, rage, fear and a sense that things will never be the same again. By the end of 2001, Jewish groups had made contributions totaling $5 million and had donated nearly $2 million to those who had been affected by the attacks (Nearly 1). Congregations across the country have continued to try to come to terms with the facts of that fateful day, through prayer, sermons (especially on the High Holidays), renewed support for Israel, and extending a helping hand to Muslims in their community.

American Jews in particular have recoiled from the outbreaks of anti-Semitism in Europe and have especially been saddened and distraught by the slaying of Wall Street journalist Daniel Pearl in Pakistan in 2002. Pearl had been kidnapped and assassinated by an Islamic terrorist group, Jaish-e-Mohammed, known for its brutality and its virulent anti-Semitism. Pearl had been snatched from the streets of Karachi in part because he was an American journalist, but in large measure because he was also Jewish. "My father is a Jew, my mother is a Jew, and I am a Jew"—those were the words his captors reportedly forced Pearl to repeat again and again, videotaping him denouncing his family, his country and his religion before suddenly slitting his throat on camera (Klaidman 1).

American Jews have also been caught up in the domestic struggle to balance national security with the individual protections afforded by the Bill of Rights. Attorney General John Ashcroft is at the center of these conflicts, which have resulted in the curtailing of freedoms in order to remain vigilant. The military tribunals that would be called to try-suspected terrorists have caused a number of Jewish civil libertarians to protest that it gives the government unlimited authority, with no person or institution in place to whom the administration is responsible. Psychologist and writer Francine Klagsbrun also has called into question the way the government has detained immigrants for questioning without releasing the names and details about the men and women who were being held (Klagsbrun 1). Some civil libertarians, a number of them Jewish, have expressed concern that in the aftermath of September 11, President Bush and Ashcroft were leading the country "toward a new McCarthy era" (Klagsbrun 2).

American Jews are particularly sensitive to issue of civil liberties. They have a biblical history to remind them of the toll that slavery exacts, and a more recent one extending back only a few generations to refugees who fled pogroms of Eastern Europe and to family members who were stripped of freedom, identity and life by Nazi Germany. The United States, a nation of laws, guaranteed certain freedoms, and Jews have held fast to the security and benefits that have flowed from such freedoms. Jews have stood with others as guardians and champions of our national civil rights, in part because the history and the culture of Jews is so centered on the need for social justice. Thus, the critical conflict between balancing American freedom against security after the September 11 terrorist attacks is one that touches many Jews in a profound way.

Like most other Americans, Jews have found themselves on both sides of the issue. Some, such as attorney Bruce J. Terris, have argued on behalf of profiling. Selecting Arab males for intense inspection before they board an airplane is both prudent and a matter of common sense, Terris wrote in a *Commentary* essay. Because "future terrorist attacks are likely to be committed by Arabs," and "all 19 of the hijackers who crashed the four planes on September 11 were Arabs," it seems like a reasonable way to proceed (Terris 1). Other critics have argued that documentary producer Steve Emerson, who produced a film exposing Islamic terrorist groups in the United States well before September 11, also had been quick to speculate that Muslim extremists had carried out the bombing in Oklahoma City in 1995 (Klaidman 16).

The point is argued that terrorists "win" when they manage to destroy "the fabric of the societies they target," which in no small measure includes our human liberty (Klaidman 17). As one author cites, Benjamin Franklin once noted, "Those who would give up essential liberty, to gain a little temporary safety, deserve neither liberty nor safety" (Klaidman 17).

The consensus among many writers is that September 11 changed the world we inhabit. One such change has been the near unity of Israel and the United States, especially on the need to combat terrorism. But one price of that closeness may be a widening of anti-Israel, anti-Semitic and anti-American sentiments in Europe, and perhaps, to a lesser extent, in the United States. At this point in American history, however, Jews in the United States are neither marginal nor outsiders. How they deal politically with the post–September 11 climate and the new security outlook of the federal government is of considerable interest to both political parties in the United States, and to all the parties in Israel.

Conclusion

The connection between American Jews and the state of Israel has been an evolving but always supportive one, shifting in reaction to the politics of each period in recent history.

While scholars have pointed out that there has never been a singular Jewish response to Israel, this chapter suggests that in periods of crisis, nearly all American Jews recognize their connection to Israel. When crises have threatened the validity of the Jewish state, the Six Day War in 1967 and the Yom Kippur war of 1973 are two examples, American Jews have repeatedly pooled their resources in support of Israel. Volunteering, fundraising and lobbying for assistance demonstrate just some of the ways in which American Jews have shown their allegiances. Although Jewish organizations and young people in the Unites States were becoming more secular, protecting and rebuilding Israel in response to crisis served as a rallying and unifying point for American Jewry.

By the same token, this chapter documents a decline of Jewish identification during much of the 1990s, thanks in some measure to divisions among Orthodox, Conservative and Reform sectors of the American and international Jewish communities. Scholars such as Wertheimer believe that individual issues, such as Jonathan Pollard's spying incident, as well as a perceived paucity of religious pluralism in Israel, all serve to rationalize the disenchantment with Israel felt by some sectors of the American Jewish community during this period.

Nonetheless, as we have shown, American Jews in the 1990s continued to have an impact on the United States government and its policies toward Israel. From the late 1960s on, the prominence of Israel within the Middle East has contributed to a sense that the interests of Israel and the United States were similar. With anti-Semitism largely on the decline in America throughout the second half of the 20th century, Jews found themselves with greater access to positions of power and influence in medicine, law, media, education and government. While not all American presidents favored Israel or the idea that Israeli and United States interests coincided, by the time of the Clinton administration, White House consultations with leaders of Jewish organizations had become common practice whenever Middle East issues were on the table.

On September 11 the United States experienced terrorism first-hand, and the strategic interests of Israel and the United States arguably have been brought closer. Commentators in the United States media and government drew strong comparisons to the

September 11 terrorist attacks and the daily battles with which Israelis live. Not everyone, however, shared this view. Opposition to Israel increased after the attacks among Americans who support Palestinian causes, and some believe that this opposition metamorphosed into anti-Semitism, particularly in parts of Europe and on some American college campuses. Other Jewish leaders and social science researchers argue, by contrast, that anti-Semitism has been rarer than imagined.

What is not in doubt is that Jews responded to the September 11 attacks as other Americans did, unifying in support of the war on terrorists and in opposition to bigotry against minority groups in the United States. And, as in the past, when Israel found itself in a state of crisis, American Jews have united to support the state financially, emotionally and politically.

Chapter Three

EDUCATION:
Experiential Learning and Jewish Education Beyond the Classroom

The daughter of a Nobel Prize-winning physicist tells the story of her father's Jewish education as part of the family's immigrant history. Born early in the 20th century as the son of East European immigrants, he grew up in Brooklyn, N.Y. He earned a doctorate in physics before going on to work at Los Alamos during World War II, teach at university and, eventually, win the Nobel Prize.

But he remembered coming home, when he was about 10, with his report card in hand. His mother stood at the door, ready to examine his grades. "Ninety-seven in English," she said accusingly. "Ninety-seven, that's a pretty good grade," he replied. "Ninety-seven is for the *goyim*," she answered. "You're a Jew and you're supposed to get 100," she said, sweeping him into the room and slamming the door behind him. He always told the story with a laugh, but that memory was seared. It captured the sense for him of the inextricable link between family and education and just how essential a role the two played for Jews in America.

Last year, in writing about this topic, we stated, "Jewish education has never been healthier; however, a sense of crisis exists." Concern over this "sense of crisis" has been growing steadily, and some Jewish professionals presently fear that, if changes in education aren't imminent, the results for Jews in terms of cultural identity could be catastrophic.

We will discuss this plight as educators and Jewish leaders view it. They have come to recognize that Jewish success in the United States, leading to Americanization for many, has been accompanied by a concomitant falling away from Judaism. As part of this departure, traditional Jewish education has dropped below other, more "American" considerations in priority. As a result, educators are having difficulty affecting change, in part because Jewish Americans today have little familiarity with Hebrew, Judaism and Jewish history and culture.

Commentators have pointed out that Hebrew schools generally play a utilitarian role, preparing boys and girls for their bar/bat mitzvahs but otherwise providing little in the way of either pleasure or knowledge. In addition, the modern Jewish household tends to prize achievement, success and acceptance in the mainstream American culture over Jewish education, which seems, almost, to run counter to these goals It sometimes appears that Jewish education is treated with little more than tolerance, something to be endured until the age of 13, when Jewish education ceases. This mind-set has been strengthened and exacerbated by the less than stellar reputation of many Hebrew schools.

One potential cause for this poor reputation is that Jewish decision-makers, men and women of wealth and influence in the United States, are not generally involved with Jewish education. Rather, they tend to be drawn to elite American private schools and universities. Moreover, older models of Jewish learning programs no longer hold as much appeal now that American Jews are no longer marginal outsiders but have become more integrated into mainstream American society.

Despite its past record, however, Jewish education is viewed by some communal leaders as potentially the best remedy for changing what they perceive as the weakening presence of Jewish identity in the United States today. While critics suggest that this estrangement of Jew and Judaism may be due, in part, to the weak Jewish educational system, proponents point out that it therefore holds the answer implicitly; if failure was the cause of the problem, its success should serve as part of the solution.

In this chapter, we will focus on experiential education, gaining skill or knowledge through activity or practice, something that many educators view as the best approach to solving this problem. The experiential education movement has generated a number of studies and experimental models. This approach is not limited to classroom learning—studies have looked at synagogue efforts, at the effects of Jewish camp experiences, and at college-based programs. The emphasis throughout is on effective learning and the need for support from a community, whether it comes from friends, fellow temple members or other students.

Several studies have focused on an encounter with Israel as part of experiential learning. In one instance, the researcher, functioning as a participant observer, accompanied a group from a local synagogue. In another, a critic reports on the early effect of Birthright Israel, the concept initiated by Edgar Bronfman and Michael Steinhardt to finance Jewish young people on their first trip to Israel. Two academicians also instituted a survey designed to guide the Birthright Israel founders. This survey, reported here, outlines the profiles of American Jewish young people ages 16 to 26 and suggests areas of divergence between Jewish and American concerns and interests.

Based on these and similar studies, many Jewish educators have come to the conclusion that Jewish education needs to be reinvigorated, that day schools require community support and reinforcement, and education/identity is an ongoing process that accompanies the act of living Jewishly. At the end of this chapter, we will present and discuss two models proposed to deal with these concerns.

Jewish Education: Conflicts

Jewish education has been an anomaly in the lives of American Jews, leaving many with a "love-hate relationship" with what is characterized as traditional Jewish learning in the classroom (Reimer 11). On the one hand, many Jewish families consider it a necessary part of the tradition for their children to study and complete their bar/bat mitzvahs at age 13. It is expected and approved as a necessary Jewish ritual. The route for this is through supplementary education, which is usually instruction at a Hebrew school often affiliated with the synagogue and aimed at children ages 11 and 12. But the experience for many Jewish children has been a negative one: the learning neither joyful nor incorporated into a Jewish life. Once the bar/bat mitzvah is concluded, Jewish education is usually over, particularly in the households of Jews whose relationship to the traditions of Judaism is minimal (Reimer 12).

By most accounts, this form of education has been deemed faulty and ineffective (Reimer 13). When compared to the pull that American education has exerted on the lives of American Jews—as a gateway to material success and acceptance by the American majority—Jewish education provides little lasting knowledge and, most important, does not reinforce the goals of Americanization (Ritterband 377-391). In this respect, it "exposes the root ambivalence of contemporary Jewish life" (Elazar 396).

Meeting Jewish educational needs is, therefore, a top priority for Jewish professionals and community leaders. The conflict is not over education alone; rather it is also focused on identity and the tension that accompanies a Jewish role in American life. Jewish aspirations for success in the wider society, viewed as acceptance and integration into American institutions, are contrasted with the urgent need for Judaism and/or Jewish identity to survive. Are Jews a part of America or apart from America (Maisel and Forman 121-139)?

The question posed above is central to Jewish organizations. Jewish professionals believe survival is at stake unless those lacking in a strong Jewish identity and/or those who have little knowledge and contact with Jewish traditions and experiences can be reached. A revised and reinvigorated approach to Jewish learning, according to some Jewish leaders, is seen as the best route to guide Jews back to Judaism (Reimer XI-XVIII). Others have something apart from religious belief in mind; they are in pursuit of methods and programs that will help forge a strong link to Jewish identity and ethnicity (Yacobi 30-44). Most community leaders agree that Jewish education is important here, whether religious Judaism, cultural identification or some combination of those two aims is the goal.

But there is a central difficulty in moving forward. The late professor Daniel Elazar, who was president and founder of the Jerusalem Center for Public Affairs, concluded that the "character of the commitment to Jewish education" was complex, if not contradictory. It was certainly ambiguous in the mind of wealthy Jewish leaders and decision-makers, many of whom sought only quality, secular American education for their children. That ambiguity is "one reason why major decision-makers rarely play any real role in the educational field and why professional Jewish educators are not major decision-makers in the [Jewish] community" (Elazar 396). According to Elazar, integration into the "cosmopolitan culture" is linked to survival and advancement for Jewish Americans, and so the American model of education, not the Jewish one, is embraced. Students and intellectuals, professionals in law and medicine, and the new generation of corporate executives who are drawn to an American way of life seek this integration (Elazar 396). They are committed to elite American educational centers, for the education that is offered and the networking often necessary for career advancement. Jewish education, whether it be part-time lessons for the bar/bat mitzvah or attendance in a full-time Jewish day school, "requires a greater measure of commitment to the notion that Jews are different and must educate their children to be different" than many American Jews are willing to accept (Elazar 396).

The result of this split between Jewish community leaders and Jewish educational professionals has led to an unusual dichotomy. The typical bell-shaped curve that might chart the ebb and flow of Jewish involvement in Jewish day schools reveals a "camel-backed shape" (Ritterband 378). It suggests that while more children than ever are attending Jewish day schools (the increase in the numbers is impressive), more Jewish Americans at the same time are intermarrying, turning secular and expressing little interest in Judaism or knowledge of the Jewish tradition (Ritterband 378). It is this falling away that has alarmed Jewish education professionals and organizations and has resulted in a series of calls to develop educational strategies that will enhance Jewish identity. The findings suggest that Jews who have had more extensive and intensive Jewish educational experiences tend to have stronger identities—showing that Jewish education does work (Reimer XII).

The problem is that while Jewish education is seen as the last "bulwark against assimilation," (Reimer XII), it is also perceived as less than excellent. There are several reasons for this, beyond competition with the quality secular day schools that are open to Jewish children of the upper-middle and upper classes. For example, there is difficulty in attracting first rate-teachers and maintaining high academic standards. Also, for students who attend Jewish school as a part-time supplement to their general education, there is the competition for the very limited resource of leisure time. Tennis lessons, music lessons, computer games and other popular culture pursuits can overshadow a call to Jewish traditions.

It is not clear, particularly in secular households, that Jewish education matters beyond functioning as a "vaccination paradigm" against assimilation. Often American Jews send "their children to Jewish schools in the hope that they would be 'inoculated' against the dreaded disease of 'assimilationitis' later in life. And, like most vaccinations, they have expected the experience to be relatively brief, largely passive, somewhat painful and administered by experts who possess arcane knowledge that the average patient does not need to possess" (Reimer XIII).

Despite some of its negative associations, Jewish education continues to serve as a way of maintaining distance from complete integration into the American social structure. Its *raison d'etre* appears to proclaim instead that Jews are a people apart from mainstream society. That was sufficient through World War II, when "social boundaries kept Jews in the fold." But once Jews moved beyond the founding Episcopalians in terms of formal education and per capita income, and particularly when they became leaders of elite institutions in the United States, the social boundaries began to disappear (Gordis and Ben-Horin 69-80).

This disappearance of social boundaries has led to a rethinking of Jewish education by some of the Jewish communal professionals. Jewish studies, in the words of one professional, are "what Jews do to be Jewish, not to become Jewish" (Reimer XIV). It is a lifelong involvement.

Experiential Education

Educational content, leading to a strengthened Jewish identity, needs a context (Marantz XV), namely the nurturing support and reinforcement of a Jewish community. It is not something that usually occurs in a classroom or in isolation (Yacobi 30-40; Grant "Planned and Enacted ..." 63-81).

A relatively new direction that is being championed as a way of achieving this goal—Jewish education seen in a positive light and connected to community and identity—is Jewish experiential education. Whether as a supplement to Jewish day school programs or as a nontraditional form of education available to everyone, Jewish experiential education has begun to attract the attention of many Jewish professionals.

Experiential education has actually been in practice since the days of John Dewey, professor of educational philosophy at Columbia University, in the first quarter of the 20th century. One of its major tenets was directed toward meeting the needs, interests and identity of the student. Its practical application took different forms at the different educational levels, according to Gene Lichtenstein, a former consultant to the United States Office of Education. For example, Montessori schools for very young children featured play, learning and structural habits. Experimental private boarding schools, such as the Putney School in Vermont and the Verde Valley School in Sedona, Arizona, offered students the opportunity to be part of a democratic community. Also, colleges, such as Antioch in Yellow Springs,

Ohio, Goddard in Plainfield, Vermont and Northeastern University in Boston, Massachusetts, incorporated work-study programs as part of the academic experience. These programs combined a term of study, then a term of work, usually off–campus, and study-abroad programs, which are now offered to students by many universities, including the University of Southern California.

Following the path of professional schools of medicine, law, education and journalism, universities also have adopted internship or apprentice programs for students, so as to provide opportunities for work in the broader community in which the school is located. They include such community based projects as mentoring students, working with social welfare agencies, and joining environmental programs. USC, for example, has a wide range of such opportunities for its students.

These experiential approaches to education in academic settings have their counterparts in informal, nontraditional programs offered by religious groups, such as the Quakers and the Mormons. The former group sends students to live and work with poor populations, such as Native Americans living on reservations, and the latter asks its members to serve for several years as missionaries abroad. Civil rights organizations also recruited students, many of them Jewish, to register voters in African-American Mississippi communities in the mid-1960s. It is no statistical accident that of the three young men lynched by members of the Ku Klux Klan in Philadelphia, Mississippi in 1964, two were Jewish, Andrew Goodman and Michael Schwerner, and one was African-American, James Chaney.

The attraction of Jewish professionals (e.g., educators, psychologists, rabbis, social workers and camp directors), to the concept of Jewish experiential education is not surprising given its stated aims: to extend knowledge of the Jewish tradition; to create a sense of community; and to aid in the process of clarifying Jewish identity while being supportive (Reisman X). Similarly, linking Jewish learning with the experience of functioning as a Jew in a special community—such as at a Jewish summer camp or a kibbutz in Israel, in an elder-hostel program or a drama group producing Jewish-themed plays, or even working on a Jewish newspaper—has seemed a practical and relevant way of communicating with contemporary Jews about their Jewish identity.

One of the early leaders in the field of Jewish experiential education was Walter Ackerman. He was raised and educated in Boston at the Boston Latin School and at a Talmud-Torah school. He attended Harvard University and the Hebrew Teachers' College of Boston, graduating *cum laude* from both in 1950 (Marantz XIII). Ackerman combined teaching in Israel and directing a camp and summer school in New Hampshire that was run by the Hebrew Teachers' College in Northwood, New Hampshire. Later he was director of the first Hebrew day school of the Conservative movement in Belle Harbor, New York, and then moved to the Hebrew Teachers' Institute at the University of Judaism in Los Angeles. Ackerman always maintained the dual positions of a teacher within a traditional school and a director of a Jewish summer camp. In Los Angeles the summer camp was Camp Ramah, which would qualify as a nontraditional educational experience. In his view, classroom and camp reinforced one another; they were each part of a communal experience and each integrated into learning. Eventually, Ackerman made *aliyah*, moving to Israel in 1973, where he was associated with the Ben-Gurion University of the Negev (Marantz XIV).

Ackerman's contributions as a teacher were manifold, and his influence was felt by many of his students and fellow teachers. The point he continued to emphasize—and which became a cornerstone of Jewish experiential education in the early 1970s— was that "one cannot understand one particular event in Jewish history or some Jewish practice or some prayer, or some ritual, *in isolation* [sic]" (Marantz XV). Ackerman stressed that it was necessary to relate all learning to its Jewish and non-Jewish contexts. Thus, for example, the Zionist movement had to be understood in light of earlier Jewish history as well as in its contemporary setting. At the same time, particular curricula had to be evaluated against the background of who was teaching and who was being taught. In more general terms, he flagged the question: What is the nature of education itself?

In secular American education today, one school of thought argues that learning particular events or traditions in isolation is not an effective way to teach or learn. Its Jewish counterpart can be found in the thinking of Jewish educators as diverse as Walter Ackerman (Marantz), Jonathan Woocher (Reimer) and Lisa D. Grant (Grant "Planned and Enacted..."), among others. They maintain that learning about or developing a Jewish identity generally requires a community to provide feedback, nurturing and support. It is an approach that has found a positive response from many Jewish educators, social workers and other professionals. In no small measure, the specific programs that have evolved during these past 30 years have shaped that response.

A Variety of Contexts

In the years after World War II, experiential programs held great appeal for Jewish professionals, including educators, rabbis, social workers and Jewish day school administrators. Subsequently, in the 1960s, many Jews were drawn particularly to experiential education, where they could apply some of its concepts and principles to Jewish learning. Its appeal was that it could be used in every educational setting-with pre-school children, parents and seniors (Tickton Schuster and Aron and Grant "Planned and Enacted..."); in formal academic learning situations and nontraditional summer camp programs (Zelon); and in educational exchanges that brought Jewish children to Israel and Israeli children to the United States (Chen). In different settings, and with different approaches, the Jewish professionals were coping with what they perceived to be a central problem: how to impart a sense of Jewish identity to American Jews who had little knowledge, experience or contact with Judaism and/or Jewish traditions (Reisman and Darvick).

Most professionals recognized that Jewish identity was not something that could effectively be taught in a classroom alone. It needed context, reinforcement, community support and family involvement (Reiman, Reisser and Yacobi). Here John Dewey, acknowledged as one of the founding fathers of experiential education, serves as a general guide: "Mere activity does not constitute experience," he wrote (Intrator and Rosov 5). Experience, for Dewey, involved relationships, between an act and its consequences, a passage learned and its application or connections to a larger world and, most important, to the student's frame of reference (Intrator and Rosov 5).

The task for Jewish educators, adapting Dewey, is to link learning with identity, and experience with communal and family interactions. The "students" in many instances are "Jews searching for a way to live Jewishly: Jews who had it and lost it, Jews who never had it and want it, converts who have chosen and are determined to make good their commitment" (Darvick 66). It is why many rabbis are drawn to the fold of experiential education.

Rabbi Debra Orenstein, spiritual leader of Congregation Makom Ohr Shalom in Tarzana and Westwood, California, is one such educator. She incorporates small learning exercises into the details of everyday life. She suggests ways that a new synagogue member may say a blessing over his or her food. When helping youngsters learn to tie their shoes, she "gives them the honor of tying the Torah scrolls together during the children's Torah service so their new skill is used in a Jewish setting" (Darvick 66).

Dr. Ron Wolfson, vice president of the University of Judaism in Los Angeles, looks for simple gestures to incorporate into one's routines. He has noted that Jewish families have adopted the Orthodox custom of blessing their children on Shabbat, but for some Jewish families that feels uncomfortable and a bit foreign. Wolfson suggests adaptation and modification. "He encourages parents to hold their kids in their laps and give them a hug or stand with their arms around their child in a family sandwich" (Darvick 68).

Risa Gruberger, director of the Whizin Institute for Jewish Family life at the University of Judaism, believes the entire family needs to participate in living Jewishly. According to Gruberger, this is the learning experience, whether it follows scriptures or is a personal adjustment that suits the family. The goal, she says, "is to create a home where you feel Judaism throughout." The learning is internalized from the soccer field to the kitchen, reinforced by others and becomes part of a lifelong process and an opportunity for Jewish meaning (Darvick 66). These are all forms of effective learning that have been incorporated into the nontraditional exploration of Jewish experiential learning.

The experiential mode has a particular appeal for adult learners, who often are self-directing. As Drs. Diane Tickton Schuster and Isa Aron have stated, adults often want "their learning to be applicable to life situations" (Tickton Schuster and Aron 44). Dr. Schuster is director of the Jewish Lives/Jewish Learning Project of the Center for Educational Studies at Claremont Graduate University in Claremont, California. Dr. Aron is a professor of Jewish education at the Hebrew Union College-Jewish Institute of Religion and Rhea Hirsch School of Education in Los Angeles. Their experience has convinced them that learning, particularly among adults, best occurs when people engage in discussions in pairs or in groups, which allow multiple perspectives to be revealed. The point, they agree, is for the learner's experiences to "illuminate the lessons of text and allowing the text to illuminate our life experiences" (Tickton Schuster and Aron 43).

Tickton Schuster and Aron's research suggests that adults benefit greatly from collaborative study. In one experiment, rabbis chose to discuss ancient Jewish texts by describing how they, the rabbis, had been affected by the books they were reading: How their behavior was changed; or insights were gained by opening their own rabbinic lives to the historical texts (Tickton Schuster and Aron 46). Their goal, as experiential educators, in working with adult members of a congregation is to create a community of learners. "The end point is not to become an educated Jew, but a continually learning one, and to go on to teach others" (Tickton Schuster and Aron 46).

Experiential education has taken on a different form within a traditional school setting. Some day schools, such as the Milken School at Stephen S. Wise Temple in Los Angeles, have incorporated weekly communication and sharing with children in an Israeli classroom in Tel Aviv. Exchanges of letters and information between the computer pals and sharing journals and experiences became a part of the weekly learning process. It was reinforced when the American children made a trip to Israel and the Israeli children to Los Angeles to live with host families. The Jewish day schools also incorporated rituals and holidays into the life and texture of classroom work, sharing the religious experiences and creating an extended family of peers. These became seamless, experiential parts connected to the more traditional academic lessons.

College is another matter. "Veering away from parental expectations is the norm among college students" (Belitsky 36). Students entering college are embarked on a journey to separate from their families and to develop their own identity. At times, this means exploring different religions or dropping earlier connections to either Judaism or an active Jewish life. This is a pattern that develops more easily if neither close friends nor roommates are Jewish, although strong family ties to Judaism can disrupt the pattern.

Jewish campus organizations such as Hillel attempt to fulfill the role of a surrogate family. Everything from the Internet, which lists Jewish activities, to campus programs such as Jewish dancing, intellectual forums, internships with Jewish organizations and sponsored trips with peers to Israel, are designed to link students together in an extended Jewish family. Hillel helps students celebrate Jewish traditions and holidays and provides the Jewish experiential education that presumably will connect students to their identity as Jews. The hope is that students will find reinforcement for an identity as Jews by seeking out *Shabbat* services, finding a Jewish mentor or connecting with other Jewish students in their dormitories, sororities and fraternities (Belitsky 36).

Another program affiliated with USC and other colleges is the Michael Steinhardt Jewish Campus Service Corps program. It is "an organization that sends recent college graduates around the country to set up pizza parties, informal lunches and phone contacts so that Jewish students can come together without fearing they won't measure up Jewishly" (Belitsky 38).

These Jewish campus programs are competing for time and attention with programs that have a secular identity and are linked with the wider American culture. The competing programs are often tied to future professional goals such as interning with a congressman, working as a summer apprentice on a newspaper or newsmagazine or serving as a tech assistant in a biological laboratory.

Chabad also maintains a campus presence at approximately 35 colleges in the United States, Canada and Great Britain. Chabad, although a Hasidic form of Judaism, is open to unaffiliated Jewish students and brings a kind of Judaic zest to the celebration of Jewish holidays and traditions. "Fifty percent of the students who join my family for *Shabbat* meals are unaffiliated," says Rabbi Eli Brackman, director of the Chabad Jewish Student Center at Maryland (Belitsky 38).

Chabad also takes a nonjudgmental and non-ideological stance toward Jews who walk through its doors. As one student in Belitsky's article remarked: "I can ask questions about religion and not feel uncomfortable, and observance is never pushed at us" (Belitsky 38). The result often is a mix of traditional Hasidic Jews and nonobservant hipsters. As Rabbi Lawrence Hoffman (who has no Chabad connection), professor of liturgy at the New York School of Hebrew Union College, explained: "The problem for most people is that they feel infantilized when it comes to religion.... Society has taught them they are not competent religiously ... and so they're guilty, they're afraid" (Darvick 88). Chabad's open-armed acceptance is reassuring for many Jewish students with little background in Judaism.

On a more academically traditional level, colleges also sponsor summer programs, some of which offer Jewish student internships with Jewish organizations, such as the America Israel Public Affairs Committee, Jewish newspapers, or at the Brandeis Collegiate Institute in Southern California. Others sponsor summer Israel experiences for study at the Pardes Institute of Jewish Studies in Jerusalem or work programs on a kibbutz. These all come under the heading of either extracurricular activities or Jewish-focused experiences, some of which are offered for college credit.

The Problem for Jewish Camps

While Walter Ackerman emphasized the dual relation of camp and classroom, Jewish educators find themselves today engaged in communal debates on the subject of Jewish camps. Jewish professionals see the camps as powerful shapers of Jewish identity. Yet camp leaders complain that Jewish camps are viewed as the stepchild of Jewish programs. Facilities are inadequate, money is scarce and support is minimal (Zelon 64). There are 750,000 Jewish youths eligible for nonprofit Jewish camps and only 30,000 attend; this constitutes only four percent. It is true some are turned away for lack of space, while others cannot afford the cost, which is $1,800 to $4,000. But despite studies that show the effectiveness of Jewish camping experiences, Jewish philanthropists and Jewish federations have given low priority to the camping experience (Zelon 66).

The camps are in trouble in part because funds have not been provided to keep them up to date with other competitive American summer camp programs. It is difficult to find and afford qualified staff members, and facilities have jumped in price, with the camps constantly falling behind. According to writer Helen Zelon, the Jewish philanthropic community in the past has been Israel-focused and so has slighted American-based programs. Moreover, there is now constant competition from summer academic programs offered by colleges, further depleting the number of Jewish youths attending Jewish summer camps (Zelon 64-67). The appeal of these peer-based American programs, combined with the elimination of quotas and barriers excluding Jewish students, have increased the difficulties of Jewish summer camps.

In spite of the competition and lack of resources, the data on Jewish camps is impressive: Children who attend Jewish summer camps overwhelmingly come home with a stronger sense of Jewish identity. Jewish campers tend to marry Jews, retain membership in synagogues, place a greater premium on Jewish rituals, and keep kosher (Zelon 82-85).

Given these results, why aren't Jewish philanthropists supporting the camping scene? First, Israel and Jewish day schools still attract most of the available funds. But most important, summer camping has never touched the lives of the affluent Jews who have become community leaders (Zelon 66). They do not send their children to camps, especially not to nonprofit summer camps, in part because it is outside their experience, but largely, according to Rabbi Ramie Arian, of the Foundation for Jewish Camping in New York, "because the quality of the programs is thought not to be up to the quality of the private camps" (Zelon 84).

Michael Steinhardt, a Jewish philanthropist who helped start the Birthright Israel program that sends young Jews ages 18 to 27 to Israel (Troy 55), understands the importance of Jewish camps, but he has had no experience with them. He never attended, nor have any of his children. "My kids had camp experiences, but not Jewish camps. We weren't smart enough. Looking back, the kids' summer camp experiences were worthless. We missed the chance" (Zelon 66). Nevertheless, camping is not a program he is actively supporting today.

Other families look to specialized private camps in the arts, music, wilderness training and computer science. Camp is seen from an American class perspective, not through a Jewish one. In the constant tug between Jewish life and an American life, summer camps and/or summer educational programs are identified more with getting ahead in America.

There have been some recent changes. Steven Spielberg's Righteous Persons Foundation has given the Jewish Foundation for Camping $180,000, and Elisa and Robert Bildner, a Jewish family in New Jersey, have set up a foundation devoted entirely to Jewish camping, starting with a $2,000,000 seed grant. The foundation has also donated $200,000 since its inception to 20 Jewish camps in North America. However, these are still just a few voices (Zelon 95).

Israel and Experiential Education

It has been an article of faith among Jewish professionals and leaders that a visit to Israel is one of the more effective ways of forging a sense of Jewish identity (Grant "Planned and Enacted..." 63). One finding by a Jewish educator was that many American Jews are hoping to discover "new possibilities in how they see their lives" (Reisman 46).

Dr. Lisa D. Grant, assistant professor of Jewish Education at Hebrew Union College-Jewish Institute of Religion, came to a related conclusion. She accompanied an American rabbi and a group from his Conservative congregation to Israel. She observed that "though they may seek out and encounter vastly different experiences of Israel, many are after an answer to the same questions: 'Where do I belong?' 'What is my place in this story of the Jewish people' " (Grant "The Role of Mentoring..." 46)? They were seeking to find a narrative about themselves and the Jewish people, a point of connection and a more solid, firmer sense of their identity as Jews, she concluded.

These studies and others suggest why Jewish experiential education is the learning model that professionals seek for middle-aged adults and younger Jews in their teens and early 20s who embark on an Israel experience. It is an approach to learning more concerned with process and effect than with information and pedagogy. It requires group interaction or one-to-one interaction with a mentor or leader, rather than a teacher leading or passing out facts to learners (Grant "The Role of Mentoring..." 47). The concern is for behavior change, not the acquisition of history and culture. Self-knowledge, not knowledge alone, is the goal. Underscoring this is the intention to create a sense of Jewish identity in some and to raise the level in others (Troy 91).

Usually these adult trips fall under the supervision of congregational leaders such as the rabbi or cantor or the educational leader of the congregation's day school. Grant found that the adults she studied all indicated they had only traveled to Israel with their congregation in the past, and that was the way they preferred to travel, at least to Israel. Nor did they see themselves as tourists, at least not as Jews traveling in Israel. They had a different, more complex purpose (Grant "The Role of Mentoring..." 51-52).

Grant found that one effect of the group trip was to help knit a closer sense of community among the members of the congregation and help establish an environment where religious identity and meaning could be explored. She found that participants sought out *Shabbat* services, whereas at home they were more casual about observing *Shabbat*; that the men wore a *kippah,* whereas at home they did not; and that one participant began to keep kosher, a result of an epiphany that he had at a service in Israel (Grant "The Role of Mentoring..." 46-57).

In one incident, a group was asked by a Jewish interpreter/ host at a visit to a Bedouin leader whether they were religious. There was a pause, which the rabbi then filled by saying "yes." The group then assented as well. Later, the rabbi explained that he had replied "yes," because it was important to him for the group to see itself as religious (Grant "The Role of Mentoring..." 52).

In a separate paper written about the same group, Grant explores how the religious experiences and the depth of identity "might be developed into lasting and meaningful life change" after returning home through a process of mentoring. She had accompanied the group to Israel as a participant observer and discovered that mentoring, which focused on individual growth, "might enhance critical reflection about one's Israel experiences and the subsequent reshaping of one's Jewish beliefs and behavior" (Grant "Planned and Enacted..." 47). She concluded that mere observations and experiences on a trip to Israel were not sufficient to lead to recognition and behavior change. Her conclusion: provide context in Israel and on the return home in the form of "ongoing dialogue and questioning... of assumptions" (Grant "Planned and Enacted..." 47).

Behavior change in adults, according to the literature, rests on a number of factors, including the interest and willingness to reflect on past experiences and eventually to build on them, while still processing new knowledge and experiences. Most important, for behavior change to occur, a particular social context is required that supports and nurtures the change.

The perpetual problem, however, is that returning home, adults usually pick up the old patterns of behavior, the luggage of daily life, and the trip becomes a source for nostalgia and pleasant recollections rather than change. "Interaction with a mentor would help participants actively reflect on their experience and shape a narrative from which they could take meaning" (Grant "The Role of Mentoring..." 54). Essentially, the mentor serves as a facilitator, but in this role may help strengthen and/or solidify Jewish identity for midlife adults along with helping to develop a connection to Israel (Grant "The Role of Mentoring..." 51). Grant believes that travel to Israel at this point in an adult's life often "is oriented toward self-actualizing experiences," and that the mentor functions as an important guide or informal tutor (Grant "The Role of Mentoring…" 51).

Birthright Israel

The concept of mentoring adults on a trip to Israel has its counterpart for young Jewish Americans in the recent Birthright Israel program. Both are responses to the unprecedented success Jews have attained these last four decades in America. In the process, that success has alarmed most major Jewish organizations and leaders, who see assimilation as a great current danger. They have made the struggle to combat it a primary goal (Ginsberg 18). Benjamin Ginsberg, professor of political science at Johns Hopkins University and director of its Center for the Study of American Government, has evaluated the conflict. "On the one hand, Jews have risen to positions of influence and leadership in America far out of proportion to their numbers." On the other, "Jewish leaders have struggled to maintain Jewish identity and distinctiveness in a nation that 'melts' its ethnic groups … into a barely distinguishable mass" (Ginsberg 4). Jewish leaders have argued that Jewish education offers a remedy, for it will stimulate communal identification (Reimer XI-XVIII).

In the past, Jewish education was a supplemental form of education, a vaccination against assimilation. However, as an effective way to impart knowledge of Jewish tradition and history, it was seen as a failure (Reimer XIII). Also, it had ceased serving as a force for kindling a Jewish identity in the competition with American popular and peer culture (Chazan and Cohen 77).

Today, American Jews—offered access not only to American institutions but also to leadership roles within those institutions— have been confronted with a major dilemma: "How long can America's Jews simultaneously lead the United States and resist assimilation by it"(Ginsberg 27)? Or, as professor Matthew Kerbel describes the conflict: How does one handle the countervailing pressures of fitting in and being different (Kerbel 122)?

The difficulty, as Jewish philanthropists Charles Bronfman and Michael Steinhardt viewed the problem, was that young Jews were fast losing the sense of being different in America. American youths lacked knowledge of Jewish history and culture, they knew no Hebrew, and they were unfamiliar with or indifferent to Israel. There were no underpinnings for a Jewish identity.

Birthright Israel was their response to this problem. Every Jew ages 18 to 27 would be offered the opportunity to visit Israel, regardless of financial status. Such a trip was seen as a form of experiential education and a strong step in the building of a Jewish identity. This would serve as the linchpin in the drive to reverse assimilation or at least create a sense of separateness and identity on the part of young American Jews (Troy 55).

Not everyone supported the program when it was first announced in 1999. Gil Troy, a Jewish professor from Montreal, Canada, was an early skeptic (Troy 54). He saw the trips as a "free exotic magic-carpet ride to the Middle East" that would just lead to another slick public relations sensation, with no lasting permanence. "Messrs. Bronfman, Steinhardt and company are offering young Jews the equivalent of free hardware," he wrote. "Jewish educators in Israel and the Diaspora must now develop the right software to make the Israel experience compatible with the realities of Jewish life, to allow Jews to process their experience in a vital and meaningful way" (Troy 56).

Before scholars evaluated the program, two professors at the Hebrew University of Jerusalem, Barry Chazan and Steven M. Cohen, consulted survey research data about contemporary American youth in an effort to suggest how the project might become most effective. They reviewed social science literature on American teenagers, specifically Jewish teens, held discussions with scholars and researchers in Israel and America, and reanalyzed the 1990 National Jewish Population survey focusing on young adults ages 19 to 26 and the parents of those 14 to 18. Their suggestions are instructive. First, they find "Jewish teens are American teens," shaped by all the forces that impinge on American young people. By and large, they are middle class, university bound, consumers of quality education caught up in the psychological dynamics and processes of adolescence. They have independent consumer spending power and their behavior and identity, Jewish and otherwise, often tend to be affected by peers, and not adults (Chazan and Cohen 77).

The two social scientists concluded there is not one homogeneous group ages 14 to 26, but rather three different age groupings: 14 to 18, 19 to 22 and 23 to 26. Each group responds to different pressures and influences and proceeds through stages of detachment from parents, while searching for a mature identity (Chazan 77). According to Chazan and Cohen, Jewish professionals divide the population in ways that serve the professionals well, but are not relevant to teenagers. The Jewish professionals see Jews as divided by denomination, or as affiliated or unaffiliated. "These distinctions may make some sense, but they mean different things for adults as opposed to younger populations" (Chazan and Cohen 80).

There may be some underestimation of Jewish youths and their Jewish interests, say Chazan and Cohen, because of using adult-oriented measures. For example, young people 14 to 26 tend not to join organizations or pay membership fees. However, lower participation rates may not mean lower interest. Moreover, many Jewish rituals that weigh Jewish identification are connected to the home, such as lighting *Shabbat* candles or observing Jewish rituals. These tend not to be followed as regularly within the setting of a dorm room at college. "The truth is that we actually have very little sophisticated knowledge about young people's Jewish beliefs, emotions, knowledge, skills and behavior" (Chazan and Cohen 80).

What is known is that about 20 percent have traveled to Israel and are highly engaged with Jewish life. These are mostly day school graduates, or Orthodox youngsters and young people with an active synagogue experience. On the other end of the spectrum, about 30 percent are young Jews with a minimum of Jewish experience and/or expressed interest. They have little Jewish background and have not visited Israel. In between is the moderately engaged group, where great gains in Israel travel might be realized (Chazan and Cohen 80).

Chazan and Cohen's survey research shows that about one quarter of American young people have visited Israel by age 26, and about one third of all Jewish American adults over 21 have traveled to Israel. Two thirds have had no experience. The result is that for many young people, visiting Israel is the exception and not the rule, and "the task being confronted is not merely to increase numbers, but to significantly change a dominant pattern that has characterized over 50 years of American Jewish life" (Chazan and Cohen 81).

These findings were viewed as challenges by Chazan and Cohen, facts and analysis the planners of Birthright Israel would need to address if they wanted to avoid failure. However, the initial reactions to the Bronfman-Steinhardt philanthropic venture were overwhelmingly favorable. More than 15,000 North American Jews ages 18 to 27 applied for the Israel travel fellowships, and 6,000 were chosen by lottery. Nearly all declared the trip to be a great success. "Blown away," "overwhelmed" and "amazed" were some of the frequent comments. "Many spoke of having felt incomplete, of having been Jewish in name only and now feeling Jewish at heart" (Troy 55).

The skeptical Troy was invited to help chair a Montreal group in February 2001 of 220 Canadians who were Israel bound. He went, he explained, because he wanted to be proved wrong: "Rather than fighting assimilation, I wanted to see young Jews embracing Judaism; rather than linking Israel with the Arab conflict, I wanted to see young Jews linking Israel with the joys of Judaism" (Troy 57). Troy found that "one of the key assumptions of the trip—that Israel works best when it is shared as a group—proved correct" (Troy 57).

For the moment, the Birthright program has been brought to a standstill. It wasn't success, failure or second thoughts that caused this; the escalating violence in the Middle East has led to cancellations across the board. "We're all devastated that we're not sending our children," said John Kaye, executive director of the Orange County Bureau of Education (Letran 1). Recently, only four families signed up to attend the bureau's six-week program to Israel. At least 25 are required for the trip. Other organizations such as Young Judea of Orange County have also seen figures plummet. Only 16 young people signed up for last summer's program; usually, it pulls in 1,200. It is not clear when Birthright Israel will resume, or what the terms of the trip will include.

Implications for the Future

There are a variety of Jewish educational models that can be examined. They range from Jewish day schools, whose numbers have increased dramatically over the past five years, to supplemental after-school Jewish programs, often at a synagogue, or attendance at a synagogue Sunday school for several hours once a week. Jewish professionals and educators have turned to these different educational programs, looking to bolster and reinforce them, as a way of furthering Jewish identity among young people. Their hope is that a strengthened Jewish education system will stem assimilation and provide a meaningful and rich environment for Jewish youths.

The day school offers the most sustained form of Jewish education, with classes in the Hebrew language, Jewish history and culture, and an overall celebration of Jewish holidays and a life lived Jewishly. However, the late professor Daniel Elazar points out day schools are of mixed quality. Some are quite serious and excellent, while others are not (Elazar 286). Some are Orthodox, while others are affiliated with a Reform or Conservative synagogue. The greater number of children by far attends through grammar school, with the figures narrowing at the high school level (Elazar 286).

In recent years, as large-city Jewish day schools have pushed for quality high school education with links to Israel and programs geared to gain admission to elite colleges, more parents have sought this alternative. The problems here are twofold: cost, which means an upper-middle-class income, and the contrast in some families between the lifestyle at home and the Jewish values and behaviors taught at school. Where the two are in sync, the issue of Jewish identity in many cases is in play—the child is rooted in a family where Jewish identity is already prized. The school reinforces these values and throws the children into a peer group where Jewish identity is valued. Secular parents are usually less involved in sending their children to the Jewish day school. When this occurs, the differences between home and school are sharpened (Elazar 286).

The supplementary programs are far leaner, in part because the hours are fewer and the commitment is less. Hebrew language is the first subject to be eliminated, because of time limitations, followed by Jewish law. What remains is something akin to Jewish national identity and loyalty, along with the utilitarian program of preparing students for bar/bat mitzvahs (Ginsberg 20).

Success is hard to come by in these circumstances. Approximately 80 percent of young Jews complete their Jewish learning by 13, without mastering Hebrew, or gaining much knowledge about Jewish history and/or culture and progressing down the road to a Jewish identity. Scholarly studies have shown that the greater the Jewish educational experience, the stronger the Jewish identity. One problem, however, has been that the quality of Jewish education has been seriously flawed (Reimer XI). It has primarily served a utilitarian communal purpose: training children to complete their bar/bat mitzvah. "American Jews do not even expect the experience to be a happy or rewarding one" (Reimer XI). Most American Jews have therefore not tended to invest seriously in acquiring a Jewish education. They have relied primarily on the public educational system, and in the last quarter century, as elite American private schools have opened their doors to Jews, upper-middle-class families have also sought out quality private secular education (Chazan and Cohen 77).

Jewish educators contend there is a need to reverse this model, converting the Jewish education into a learning experience that is more "compelling, inspiring and satisfying" (Reimer XII). Supplemental or after-hours schooling is still the predominant means by which Jewish children participate in a Jewish education. Studies suggest the key variable to success in this setting is the degree to which a congregation supplies a strong supporting role for its school. They conclude it is not the school that provides the education, but "it is the community as a whole" (Reimer XVII).

Redefining Supplemental Education

Despite the criticism, supplemental education was deemed acceptable while Jews were kept outside the social system in the United States. When social barriers against Jews were lowered, disaffiliation *and* Jewish involvement increased. This has set up divergent paths: "More committed Jews have increased their commitment, while less committed Jews have more and more opened themselves to the forces of assimilation" (Rittenband 378).

Two Jewish cultures have taken shape, not unlike in Israel. There the split is between the Orthodox and the secular; in the United States, it is between secular Jews and those who choose to live a more observant and Jewishly identified life. Rittenband describes it this way: "Jewish day schools are bursting at the seams and intermarriage rates are going through the roof" (378). The problem is exacerbated because, for many Jews, the United States is viewed as a "culturally neutral society" in which the community is seen as secular, thereby affording Jews an opportunity for access not as Jews but as American citizens (Rittenband 379). He sees Jews becoming secular in order to become American.

Arnold Eisen, professor of Jewish studies at Stanford University, who describes himself as an optimist, considers the coming decades as reinforcing the autonomy of the individual, with an emphasis on flexibility and pluralism. "Jewish lay people," he says, "seem quite happy with the notion that tradition is a legacy for them to use as they see fit, even piecemeal, rather than a coherent and binding set of obligations—let alone a belief system to which they must assent" (Eisen 454).

The question then posed for Jewish educators is: How do you redefine educational programs beyond just being experiential and nontraditional? The day schools today, despite their burgeoning expansion, have a limited number of openings and, along with their high standards and high tuition costs, are prohibitive for all but the wealthiest temple members and congregations to maintain.

Nevertheless, even with communal and Federation support, numbers are still small (Elazar 284-285). Hence, there is the focus on supplemental forms of education.

Diane Yacobi, educational director of the Jewish Community Center of Fort Lee, N.J., suggests that change requires looking at education in a different way, distinguishing between traditional and nontraditional forms of Jewish education (Yacobi 30). Nontraditional forms possess great possibility, she contends, because they are driven by a personal growth agenda and their purpose often has to do with identity development (Yacobi 30). For new directions, she urges that educators turn to cultural context, existing research in Jewish education and formal academic preparation.

Cultural context assumes great importance in her model. It concentrates on the places in which American and Jewish culture connect, while educational research studies point toward trends in religious life and leadership dynamics, all of which are needed if we are to gain insight into identity development. She concludes that we need to develop a new set of academic guidelines, which will help in training Jewish teachers (Yacobi 30-40).

Yacobi sees personal behaviors and practices as more important than an objective set of truths; a quest culture that is searching for personal direction and belief, she contends, takes precedence over religious and institutional loyalties. Jewish life today is defined by personal choices, which means including or disregarding Judaism as part of a meaningful life. There is now an alternative: inclusion in American society (Yacobi 32). Jewish identity is thus seen as an ongoing process in which the individual enters and departs in much the same way he enters or leaves a room (Yacobi 33).

Two Models

Both the strength and weakness of Jewish education today is that it is decentralized and local. Experiences are shared nationally at the Coalition for the Advancement of Jewish Education annual meetings and at the national United Jewish Communities' annual General Assembly. Studies are published in journals and informal networking of Jewish educators occurs. But each program and each attempt to remedy the national crisis of "Jewish survival" is local, unique to a particular synagogue and/or community and is not necessarily transferable elsewhere. In this sense, there is no general theory of Jewish education that addresses the problems of assimilation, limited knowledge of Jewish history and culture, and a weakened sense of Jewish identity that Jewish educators have been decrying. Nor is there a national solution or even a national remedy at hand.

However, the local nature of the Jewish educational programs attempted in different communities is well-suited to the conviction that Jewish experiential education is perhaps the best path to follow. Here the emphasis is on process, community support and feedback. Variables—such as individual need and the different role of teachers, facilitators and mentors—are dependent on the structure of a given learning situation. The general outlines of process are replicable, but the details will differ significantly. In this sense, local autonomy and custom-designed programs becomes a necessary asset.

Two models recently written about are: 1) a program at Temple Akiba, a modern synagogue-based approach to educating the congregational community (Reimer XI-XVIII), and, 2) a Reconstructionist version of Judaism, which perceives its approach and strategy as a fusion of ethnicity and ethics (Schein and Staub 207-221).

At Temple Akiba, the assumption is that the synagogue should function as the preeminent educating institution (Reimer XIV). "At its best, the synagogue, more than any other Jewish institution, can be a true educating community. Judaism is taught in a place where it is practiced, where Jewish children and especially Jewish adults can not only study Torah together, but pray and perform *mitzvot* together" (Reimer XV).

The strength of the Temple Akiba program rests on being connected to the life of a real Jewish community. The synagogue serves as an educational center and a surrogate family, a place where Jewish identity is linked to the community. The presumption is that Jewish education and Jewish community revolve around Judaism, not Jewish ethnicity (Reimer XV).

Secular Jews and unaffiliated Jews are not likely to be part of this process, whose distinctiveness lies in its approach, connecting Jewish tradition and the Torah with "the truths of their lives" (Reimer XVI). The premise is that Jewish education requires a key Jewish component—namely the tradition of Judaism as reflected through the study of the Torah—but that it becomes an academic exercise unless it relates and responds to the diverse lives of the congregation. Here the emphasis is on group process and individual experience. The teachers strive for an interactive learning experience, one based on dialogue, and the community provides feedback, support and context: "The learner is never asked to give up the standpoint of her/his experience, the ultimate criterion for making truth claims. But she/he is encouraged to look into the texts of the tradition for the experiences and reflections contained there as well" (Reimer XVI). While the key variable is the depth of support provided by the congregation, Akiba's distinctive Torah approach is always at the center of the student's life. In effect, the process is ongoing: the creation of a community where Jewish teaching and tradition is not without struggle, but where it engages the congregation members in all aspects of their lives. This is the "battlefield where the future of American Judaism will be played out" (Reimer XVIII).

The Reconstructionist model described by Jewish educators Jeffrey L. Schein and Jacob J. Staub has a different focus. It envisions Judaism as a fusion of ethnicity and ethics. The authors also believe in locating the learning in the individual; and they, too, recognize the changes that have occurred in American society over the last 50 years. Their perception is that American youths today are individualists, and that they are caught up by a different sense of Jewish self than their parents and grandparents (Schein and Staub 1-10).

Schein and Staub start from this point. Their conclusion is that young Americans feel much more at home in society today. By addressing common concerns in the learning process, the Reconstructionists hope to transcend factionalism. The aim here is to de-emphasize skills, such as information acquisition, and the content of moral virtues. Instead, primacy is given to Jewish identity. They follow the findings of Chazan and Cohen in their profile of contemporary young Americans, and they too believe that Jews need to be open to pluralism (Schein and Staub 205).

However, ethnicity comes easily, they believe. Form is everything; substance is less important. The education mission is to legitimize Jewish identification and to impart a sense of peoplehood with other Jews. That sense of peoplehood needs to be grounded in Jewish culture, history and the Hebrew language—to the particularities of Jewishness (Schein and Staub 209-210). Nevertheless, it is people's experiences that are the touchstones, not beliefs, laws or ethics (Schein and Staub 211).

The Reconstructionists come to Jewish education from a philosophical rather than a psychological perspective. It is Dewey they turn to in America, and to the sociology of knowledge. Their goal is to provide students with an experience of development, of a spiritual force in Jewish life as it manifests itself in the history of Jewish peoplehood.

Pluralism, freedom of choice, individual autonomy and the weakening of family and communal ties are all part of the structure of contemporary America (Chazan and Cohen 77). And the educational models that these Jewish experiential educators are pursuing start from these very American points of departure.

Conclusion

Education tends to be highly valued in the Jewish community. Which type of education is most valued, however, and the role it ought to play in Jews' lives, has been a topic of debate and reflection.

Throughout much of the past century, many Jews have associated their success in this country with Americanization. For them, integration and acceptance are seen as key factors to their happiness or prosperity, and thus the traditional American model of education takes on greater importance. On the other hand, some Jewish leaders have held that Jews have a fundamental responsibility to Judaism and Jewishness, and they warn that any trend toward disassociation is dangerous.

That controversy is likely to continue, and consequently, it will likely continue to be true that views about Jewish education will be hotly debated. There can be little doubt, however, as we have documented, that Jews who have the most intensive Jewish education tend to have the strongest sense of Jewish identity, and that incorporating a community into the education process enhances learning. Many scholars believe that a community of supporters is essential for a positive and effective learning environment.

That community can take many forms, as we try to show in this chapter. It can be a college Hillel group, for example, or a Jewish camp. Another example of effective experiential education can be seen in the recent trend for Jews to travel to Israel in programs such as Birthright Israel. They travel in search of an answer to the question: "Where do I belong" (Grant "Role of Mentoring..." 46)? This search is considered by many educators to be an excellent method of strengthening Jewish identity, and the group interaction provides the sense of community that proponents of experiential education find so important.

The lasting effects of such programs have been a topic of disagreement, however. Some scholars suggest that despite the close-knit community that forms, the effects of the trip are transient, fading soon after people return to the normalcy of their everyday lives. These scholars recommend that participants seek out a mentor upon return to continue the group interaction and truly make the trip a lifelong process. Researchers have raised methodological questions as well. Because the choice to go to Israel is voluntary rather than mandated, perhaps the growth and change observed in those who participate occurs not because of the trip to Israel, but because the participants were predisposed to grow and change anyway. This possibility does not diminish the efficacy of the trips for those who choose to make them; rather, it suggests that trips to Israel, while an effective method of strengthening identity for a certain subset of Jews, may not have the same effect for others.

Whatever the strengths and limitations of any particular experiment in experiential education, its viability as a method or strategy is not in question. Because it is applicable to all ages, it offers an excellent option for educators who strive to make Jewish learning a lifelong activity.

Chapter Four

IMAGE:
Artists, Museums, and the Question of "Jewish Art"

The involvement of Jewish Americans in the world of art—high and low—continues to be profound. Jews make up a sizable percentage of museum visitors, patrons and supporters, while many artists, scholars and critics are Jewish as well. Indeed, the world of art in the United States would be greatly diminished without the presence and participation of America's Jews.

Ironically, this has not been reflected in what might be called Jewish art. In the 19th century and much of the 20th, the notion of Jewish art was largely dismissed. It has only been in the last 50 years that scholars, critics and artists have grappled seriously with the question of Jewish art: Does it exist? If so, how do we define it?

This chapter will first look at ways that critics have tried to define or to avoid Jewish art. Some have focused on theme and utility of the art object, others on identity, history and cultural heritage. A Jewish spirit has been claimed for the social realism of the 1930s, which, while secular, took on the burden of defending individual rights against social upheavals in America and Europe. Meanwhile, a more spiritual, Messianic approach has been identified in the works of a number of contemporary women artists.

Inevitably, critics and scholars have been drawn into the discussion. They are the men and women who often define terms and set the agenda for how we approach our national art. As in the past, many of the critics and scholars are Jewish. In this chapter, we will discuss a new approach that incorporates the Jewish identity of the scholar/critic in the process of analyzing works of art.

We will also examine the conundrum that faces Jewish museums today. Do they function as ethnic custodians, exhibiting Jewish shows for a Jewish audience? Or do they compete for a wider audience of Americans, featuring both Jewish and non-Jewish artists and themes? As we will indicate, the challenge confronting Jewish museums today comes from the major, non-ethnic urban museums, many of whose patrons and board members are Jewish, and many of whose exhibitions feature prominent Jewish artists.

It is impossible to discuss all, or even most, of America's Jewish artists. We have concentrated on perhaps the first artist who seriously explored Jewish themes in the beginning of the 20th century, Max Weber. We have also looked at the contemporary artist R.B. Kitaj, whose paintings he defines as Jewish, reflecting the tension and conflicts he perceives in his own identity as a Jew and an outsider. We have included as well a brief discussion of some major Jewish cartoonists whose comics, illustrations and cartoons have helped define America's popular culture. We have also examined some of the controversy surrounding the *Too Jewish?* show at the Armand Hammer Museum of Art and Cultural Center in Los Angeles in 1997. We raise the question: Do the images illuminate the condition and place of Jews in American society today or do they falsify and perpetuate stereotypes?

In the final section of the chapter, we turn to future directions for the Jewish museum world, with particular emphasis on multimedia exhibitions and the use of technology to involve visitors, converting them into participants. This has been a direction that Holocaust museums have pursued. Meanwhile, scholars are still examining depictions of the Holocaust, finding new ways to analyze images and statements that persist in enveloping us and that remain powerful even today.

These are the main points we will touch upon in the chapter. In the end, they have a way of coming back to issues of identity and the question, once again, of a definition for Jewish art.

Defining Jewish Art

What is Jewish art? The question confronted Jewish art critics and historians throughout much of the last century. At first, there was a tendency to point in pride to a work painted or drawn by a Jewish artist, not unlike the way Sandy Koufax or Hank Greenberg were referred to as exemplary Jewish baseball players. But historian and former Yale professor Peter Gay (the current director of the Center for Scholars and Writers at the New York Public Library) was not persuaded that Jewish art existed solely because the artists were Jewish. The artists' Jewish identity was significant only in terms of biographical detail. There was no "Jewish way of knocking a fastball out of the park or of pitching a no-hitter" (Gay 1).

Other historians avoided biography. An art object need only suggest a link to Jewish identity or simply fill a utilitarian Jewish need as an object of ritual observance to be defined as Jewish art. After all, in the past, Jews commissioned non-Jews to create Jewish works of art (Rolnick 41).

Two prominent art critics of the mid-20th century, Clement Greenberg and Harold Rosenberg (both of whose collected papers reside in the Getty Research Institute) were "reluctant to identify a painter as a 'Jewish artist' simply on the grounds that he—or she—was indeed a Jew" (Gay 1). They feared that the label "Jewish artist" would isolate the Jewish painters and marginalize them, as well as the work, which often dominated the world art scene (Gay 1). Both critics were secular Jews.

For critics and art historians, the question of Jewish identity and art lately has taken on a more complex and urgent tone. Today, art critics/historians trying to arrive at an answer to the question "What is Jewish art" are suddenly faced with a deeper, more subjective question about their own Jewish identity in a changing, contemporary America. Critics and historians are no longer outside observers; they, and their own Jewish identity, have become part of the discussion (Soussloff 1-12).

It was not always this way. Until recently, it was assumed Jews in ancient times were incapable of artistic creation because of the 2nd Commandment's prohibition against idol worship and reproducing graven images. The result was that no single "Jewish style" ever evolved (Rolnick 41).

In the 19th to the mid-20th centuries, scholars—particularly Jewish scholars—adopted an Euro-centric approach to the study of art history and culture. Essentially this shaped the discipline of art history, so that works were viewed in terms of nationality. Given the absence of a Jewish state, this all but eliminated Jewish art from any serious consideration (Soussloff 5). Artists were French or German or Italian, and their work was linked to a period and a national identity, not an ethnic one. Nor were ceremonial art objects given much place of honor. The artifacts—the ritual objects, the coins, the books and the Judaica exhibited in Jewish museums—were viewed as marginal to the study of art and culture (Cohen "Exhibiting History..." 98). One byproduct of this scholarly assumption was to eliminate the impact of Jewish culture on the art of Europe and America. Artists and art critics who were Jewish were creating within the tradition of their nation, and thus were seen as national artists and scholars, or their work was dismissed as "oriental" (Gay 1). Being Jewish was considered irrelevant (Cohen "Exhibiting History..." 98).

An Israeli Perspective

It is not surprising then that when art historian and Israeli professor Bezalel Narkiss first began to explore the field more than four decades ago, "most scholars didn't think of 'Jewish art' as a serious field of study" (Rolnick 41). Narkiss, however, started from a relatively new vantage: He was a Jewish citizen of a Jewish nation, Israel. His intention, against the prevailing opinion, was to demonstrate that Jewish art existed. Like the Bezalel School of Arts and Crafts in Jerusalem, founded by Zionist sculptor Boris Schatz in 1906, Narkiss' Center for Jewish Art would serve as a standard-bearer for artists who would embrace a Jewish spirit in their work (Gay 1).

Professor Narkiss, winner of the Israel Prize in 1999 for his work in the field of Jewish art and founder of the Center for Jewish Art at the Hebrew University in Jerusalem in 1979, looked at the field from the vantage of a Jewish nationalist. He made his life's work the indexing of all Jewish art in the world. Obviously, there could be no single style, he concluded, because the artists were scattered across centuries as well as continents. However, their work did possess something that could be classified as a common cultural heritage. "Through art, Hasidic Jews and Reform Jews can unite," said Narkiss. "They will see that there is one culture in America and Europe. Everywhere" (Rolnick 41). And, he concluded, "to qualify as Jewish art, an object must be used by Jews or express a Jewish identity. It doesn't necessarily have to be created by a Jewish artist." For example, Narkiss refers to 19th century French impressionist Camille Pisarro as "a very good Jew." However, Narkiss adds he does not consider Pissarro's paintings of fruit to be Jewish art (Rolnick 41).

Another Israeli perspective on Jewish art can be seen in the important and critically acclaimed work of Yaacov Agam. Born in 1928, Agam is a contemporary, Israeli, self-identifying Jewish Artist. (*Contemporary Artists* 4th ed.). The son of a rabbi, Agam refers to the Biblical Hebrew outlook as the inspiration behind his art. The artist came from extremely humble beginnings and began to draw at an early age but feared repercussions because he believed that Judaism forbade the craft. Instead of anger, his father reacted with understanding and encouragement, and Agam later went to study in Jerusalem at a professional school of arts and crafts. He became committed to finding a new art form, and critics suggest that his unique approach to artistic expression

suggests he succeeded in his goal (www.agam.net/ownwords/
lifestory4html).

Secular Messianism: Male and Female Artists

Professor Matthew Baigell of Rutgers University assumes there
are "no credible answers" to the "What is Jewish art conundrum"
(Baigell and Heyd 182). Nevertheless, Baigell believes a Jewish
point of view is apparent in the work of Jewish artists of the 1930s
and is very much present in the work of those artists who began
in the 1970s to deal with the Holocaust. His disclaimer is that
the art is not "uniquely Jewish, but rather one that emerges from
a Jewish heritage" (Baigell and Heyd 182). That heritage,
according to Baigell, imparts a Messianic quality to the work of
some artists. Their art is produced in the service of helping to
create a better world.

Here the notion of *tikkun olam* (repairing the world) is clearly
stated as a goal. Baigell cites the mural projects of artists Ben
Shahn and Philip Evergood in the 1930s. Each touched on the
immigrant dreams of Americans but also pointed to Isaiah and
the idea that the future cradles the artist's dream of betterment
(Baigell and Heyd 183). Baigell does not believe that Shahn and
the other social realists of the period held a conscious Messianic
view. They were responding, however, to their Jewish heritage
by substituting a secular political doctrine for a religious one.
This secular doctrine was very much in tune with assimilation
ideals and the falling away from religion. Art became a political
weapon for them in a continuing struggle to eliminate anti-
Semitism and to alleviate Jewish marginalization (Baigell and
Heyd 184).

World War II, the Holocaust, the situation of Jews in America
in the second half of the 20th century, these historical forces
changed everything. Social realism and the secular messianism
of the 1930s all but disappeared from the art scene in the United
States, to be followed largely by abstract expressionism. However,
by the 1970s, a different Messianic strain emerged, particularly
in the work of female artists, many of whose paintings and
sculptures invoke the notion of *tikkun olam*. The link is more

spiritual than political but also reflects a secular Messianism. Art here is viewed as "part of a healing process after the Holocaust, a process that tries to control, if not eliminate, the rancor of the past" (Baigell and Heyd 186).

In short, while the earlier secularists of the 1930s ignored the whole notion of a Jewish covenant, the more recent female artists—Weisberg in Los Angeles, Edith Altman in Chicago and Renata Stein in New York, among others—express a decidedly Jewish voice in their "desire to renew the Covenant and to share Jewish testimony with the world" (Baigell and Heyd 190).

One such artist is professor Ruth Weisberg, dean of the School of Fine Arts at the University of Southern California and an advisory board member of the Casden Institute for the Study of the Jewish Role in American Life. In 1971, professor Weisberg published an artist's book with nine prints entitled *The Shtetl: A Journey and a Memorial*. The artist focused on life between the two World Wars in an Eastern European *shtetl*. She states, 'What I do feel very strongly is that my desire to make art, to create meaning, and to be generative is a conscious commitment I make to being affirmative in the face of the knowledge of great systematic cruelty and inhumanity. To remember and to affirm have for me a specifically Jewish sense of renewal. It is the part I can play in the repair of the world—*Tikkun Olam*' (Baigell and Heyd 186).

Kitaj: The Jewish Outsider

Perhaps the most self-identifying Jewish artist in the contemporary art scene is American-born artist R.B. Kitaj, who spent most of his years studying, working and living in Great Britain. Today he resides in Los Angeles. As an American and a Jew, Kitaj identified himself as an outsider in Great Britain; he stressed this by immersing himself in Jewish themes throughout his work. In a manifesto that he published, Kitaj wrote, "I must declare or confess my most complex credentials—one of the outstanding facts of my life and diasporic condition: utterly American, longingly Jewish, School of London, I spin my years away from both my heartlands" (Baigell and Heyd 224).

Professor Sander L. Gilman of the University of Illinois, a guest lecturer at the Casden Institute's 2000 forum on Jewish identity, views Kitaj's sense of being an outsider as a kind of creative displacement. It is a Jewish consciousness, says Gilman, performing in a larger world—namely, the London art world. As such, Kitaj functions as both an insider and an outsider, and it is the tension between the two that sustains much of his work (Baigell and Heyd 30, Gilman 225).

Gilman identifies Kitaj's diasporism as being "tied to a complicated 'good bad' relationship with his own Jewishness. To be a Jew was to be different; to be an artist was a way of escaping that difference" (Gilman 225). Gilman notes that the leading artists of Kitaj's generation in Great Britain were Francis Bacon, Lucian Freud, David Hockney and Kitaj himself—all gays or Jews (Baigell and Heyd 30, Gilman 225).

Kitaj is not sure what being Jewish means in the second half of the 20th century, particularly for an American expatriate living in a nation, Great Britain, that he finds anti-Semitic. But he knows that he is indelibly Jewish, in part because others see him this way but in large measure because of the Holocaust, an event that occurred in his lifetime. "What holds me in its grip, so that I can't escape its still stinking breath," Kitaj has said, "is the epochal murder of European Jews" (Gilman 228). Gilman considers this to be at one with the guilt of post-1945 Jews in America, who were never in danger. That sense of guilt today is merged with the guilt of abandoning Israel, Gilman writes. (Baigell and Heyd, Gilman 228).

The Scholars' Search for Identity

Professor Catherine M. Soussloff, the Patricia and Rowland Rebele chair in Art History at the University of California in Santa Cruz, is caught up by a parallel set of feelings that she believes affect art scholars. Referring to a study by art historian Colin Eisler, she notes that many of the German *émigrés* who fled the Nazis became the key founders of American art history in the latter half of the 20th century (Soussloff 1). Soussloff suggests in her essay "Introducing Jewish Identity to Art History" that the *émigrés* may have been influenced by three leading critics in America, all Jews: Bernard Berenson, Meyer Schapiro and Clement Greenberg (Soussloff 2). The three range from gifted writer and Renaissance authority (Berenson), to leading academic scholar (Schapiro), to influential critic of contemporary American art (Greenberg). All three downplayed the Jewish factor in most of the work they analyzed.

So, too, did the *émigrés*. Despite their experience in Germany and Austria and their reputation as well as influence on graduate students in the United States, they tended to ignore Jewish art and slide past the concept of Jewishness in their approach to art history. It was an effort, explains professor Soussloff, "to avoid the notion that their religion or ethnicity had anything to do with their art criticism"(Soussloff 2).

Today, art academics have come to recognize that their "historical subjectivities" are important to their scholarship, but it is complicated because the Jewish art historians are reluctant to deal with their own identity as it affects their criticisms (Soussloff 5). Soussloff believes that programs in African-American studies and women's studies influence current scholarship in art history. By following the path of gender and ethnic studies, art historians have come face to face with identity issues for artists, critics and patrons. In this regard, a cultural studies approach mirrors "the persistently embattled positions of minority groups in contemporary society" (Soussloff 8).

One result of this new trend in art history scholarship is an indirect rejection of the Euro-centric concept of history and society, which in the past attracted Jewish scholars on both sides of the Atlantic. Now it is the interpreter's stance, his or her biography and psychological relationship to the text, which must be dealt with when analyzing art. For Soussloff, this means coming to terms with and understanding her own Jewish identity. Not coincidentally, it raises provocative questions for her about who is a Jew and what being Jewish means in today's changing America. That is one direction that art history research in the 21st century must go, she concludes (Soussloff 9).

A Proliferation of Jewish and Other Ethnic Museums

If Soussloff and others have begun to examine the effects of Jewish identity on both artists and scholars, Jewish museums and their trustees have been faced with a different set of choices. The reality is that time produces change and museums must respond to these changes. In contemporary America, we have witnessed dynamic social shifts that have affected economic prosperity, the civil rights of minorities and the role of women in our society. In a broader and more general context, the "melting pot" image of America has been replaced by the celebration of cultural diversity. We have also seen a tremendous change in the role and acceptance of Jews in American society and the conditions of life that have followed from this.

New ways of perceiving those around us, including women, gays, African Americans and Jews, have also produced a set of "politically correct" responses. If the audience has changed, in identity as well as in response, it follows that so too must the museum transform itself. Relevance and the need to compete in the cultural marketplace demand it. In the case of Jewish museums, curators and boards of directors have had to seek out new ways of addressing criticisms aimed at their once-sacrosanct institutions; in effect, they have been forced to respond culturally to a new reality (Freudenheim 80).

Some museum scholars have sought to explore new directions with familiar objects. Mel Alexenberg, artist and dean of visual studies at Miami's New World School of the Arts, has urged that we turn again to Jewish ritual objects such as the Torah scroll or the branches of the menorah, which "lead directly to a living form of Jewish memory and experience" (National Foundation for Jewish Culture 1). Meanwhile, Dr. David Carr, associate professor of library and information studies at the Rutgers School of Communication, Information and Library Studies, wonders: "If memory follows from our most authentic experiences, how then does our memory follow in a world where so much of our experience is surrogate, mediated, virtual, given to us in pre-constructions, designed by strangers" (National Foundation for Jewish Culture 1)?

Most Jewish museums as we know them today are relatively new. The first one was built in Vienna in only 1895. New York's Jewish Museum began as an adjunct to the library of the Jewish Theological Seminary and did not come into its own as a separate museum until 1947 (Freudenheim 81). In the beginning of the 20th century, its audience was primarily the German and Sephardic Jews who were already American citizens, rather than the mass of Jewish immigrants who were streaming into the United States from Eastern Europe. Its role was more related to collecting Judaica, or archival material, than to what we today classify as art and sculpture.

By 1947, the audience had shifted to include, in large numbers, the children and grandchildren of the immigrants who had so increased the population of Jews in America. Many were now part of a new, expanding middle class who had become increasingly secular and self-identified with the culture of the United States—high and low. They wanted their museum to adopt a more elitist and American role in New York's cultural life, or at least the trustees did. A Jewish museum was seen as a manifestation of self-definition. The result: In the late 1950s and the early 1960s, in the early stages of the civil rights movement and before the women's movement or gay liberation had taken off, the New York Jewish Museum began to assert itself as a dominant cultural center for exhibiting contemporary American art, of both Jewish and non-Jewish artists. Tom L. Freudenheim—the Casden Institute's 1999 Jerome Nemer lecturer and, until recently, the director of the Gilbert Collection in London—said that indirectly, the museum's curators appeared to be "saying that we are the chosen people not only for showing the rest of you how to conduct your ethical lives, but also how to recognize the really important culture in your midst" (Freudenheim 85).

Multiculturalism Moves Center Stage

During the next 30 years, changes continued to occur and multiculturalism became the focus in the urban centers, universities and museum centers. In political terms, the idea of the melting pot began to give way to ethnic and gender identity, and that soon translated into cultural identity (Starger 1).

African Americans were one of the leading groups that began to establish this agenda as they struggled for recognition and acceptance. In the late 1960s, an official at the Metropolitan Museum of Art issued a statement explaining that the Met would exhibit black artists "if there are any" (Starger 1). This type of statement, made during a period of protests and demands for recognition, fueled the struggle to make museums more responsive to the ethnic communities within the city, and it led to particular battles within the museums themselves, especially the ethnic museums. The choices were clear: High-end art that was minimally connected to ethnicity or a strong focus on ethnic art?

In the New York Jewish Museum's early years, the emphasis had been on Jewish fine art, and history had determined the way a show was selected and organized. Then, in the late 1950s, with the role of Jews in New York considerably improved, new trustees tried to broaden the audience to non-Jews by showing the best of contemporary work by artists such as Jasper Johns, Robert Rauschenberg and Willem de Kooning, none of whom were Jewish (Starger 2).

In the decades that followed, the changes in society opened the discussion so that curators began to ponder just how ethnic representation would fit into Jewish programs. Their concern was that ethnic artists (and thus the museum) "would be consigned to a visual ghetto," filled with art objects that while ethnically correct would simply be classified as folk art or political art, narrow in focus and of dubious artistic merit (Starger 3). As Tom L. Freudenheim writes, Judaica might come to represent a form of "apologia in a temple of high art" (Freudenheim 85).

Achieving Relevance

Today, the situation has changed once again, as it undoubtedly will in the future. Jewish museums find themselves competing with a variety of cultural centers for Jewish and non-Jewish visitors. Moreover, Jews in the major urban centers, notably Los Angeles, are the backbone of the art and museum world. In Los

Angeles, this means venues such as the Museum of Contemporary Art and the Los Angeles County Museum of Art, which are deeply indebted to Jewish patrons and benefactors. It also includes two Jewish museums, the Skirball Cultural Center and the Simon Wiesenthal Center's Museum of Tolerance. The competition among all four is for funding and audience.

To compete successfully, the Jewish museums in Los Angeles and elsewhere will have to exhibit work that is much more than a prideful statement of Jewish heritage. Otherwise, Jewish museums risk becoming obsolete or once again turning inward on themselves, catering only to a narrow Jewish audience (Freudenheim 87). That audience itself will have greatly diminished as American Jews continue to integrate and assimilate into the broader American institutions, serving as trustees and board members of the major urban non-Jewish museums.

Meanwhile Jewish subjects are no longer reserved solely for ethnic museums. The Los Angeles County Museum of Art mounted an exhibition titled "Degenerate Art," that featured works the Nazis refused to exhibit. The museum also included, as highlights of its annual season, major shows devoted to the work of R.B. Kitaj and Eleanor Antin. All three could have been major exhibitions in a Jewish museum.

How then does a Jewish museum differentiate itself? At the January 1998 conference of the Council of American Jewish Museums, Rabbi Arthur Hertzberg, professor of religion at New York University, addressed the group this way: "You are not custodians of aesthetics. You are the custodians of moral and spiritual history." His was a voice raised against what he saw as a narrow, elitist art approach. In a sense, he was addressing the converted. Jewish museums have responded to the contemporary challenge by expanding their concerns. Today, they are often "both a center for cultural study and preservation and an anchor for communal education and outreach" (National Foundation for Jewish Culture 1).

His words were echoed by Margo Bloom, the director of Philadelphia's National Museum of Jewish History and co-chair of the conference: "Jewish museums can play a critical role in enhancing Jewish identity. Visits to museum exhibitions, and encounters with the artifacts that are tangible evidence of our heritage," she said, "provide a sense of connection to other Jews, across time and across space, in a powerful, immediate and completely unique way. Museums also provide places for people to gather and explore issues that are meaningful to them as Jews" (National Foundation for Jewish Culture 1).

Nevertheless, others at the conference were concerned that the Jewish museum world needed "to find ways to attract both a Jewish and growing non-Jewish public" (National Foundation for Jewish Culture 2). A return to Judaica and narrowly focused Jewish exhibits might lead the museums and their patrons down a wrong path. The issue raised at the conference is one that affected different museums in different ways, based on the communities in which they were based and the populations they served. There was no longer a national Jewish museum world in America.

In 1977, when the CAJM was initially founded by the National Foundation for Jewish Culture, there were only seven members. By 1998, there were 55 institutions in 21 states and Canada (plus a host of Jewish museums in Europe). The membership today includes "art and history museums, Jewish historical sites, Jewish historical and archival societies, Holocaust centers, synagogue museums, Jewish Community Center galleries and Jewish student center galleries" (National Foundation for Jewish Culture 2). Each has its own particular focus.

The Skirball Cultural Center, for example, has sought a solution to the problem of differentiation by appealing to the Jewish and non-Jewish communities of Los Angeles. The museum's centerpiece is a collection that concentrates on the Jews who came to America. However, mindful of its role in Los Angeles, it has featured shows celebrating Latino Heritage month along with exhibitions of contemporary Jewish artists such as *The History of Matzoh: The Story of the Jews* by the late artist Larry Rivers (Soll 1-2). Keeping Jewish identity at its forefront, the center in effect has attempted to emulate New York City's 92nd Street Young Men's Hebrew Association (YMHA), where

Jewish curators and directors provide a cultural window onto the city. While Jewish America is the main concern, the YMHA also attempts to be inclusive, scheduling art shows and performers who reflect the different identities of the broader New York community. These include poetry readings by Mark Strand and John Ashberry and political discussions about the guilt or innocence of the late Alger Hiss.

This is just one approach—a mix of popular and traditional culture that fittingly takes place in New York and Los Angeles. Freudenheim suggests that Jewish museums might also look to an additional role, by offering exhibitions that connect Jewish experience to matters of social injustice (Freudenheim 90). This is a direction the Simon Wiesenthal Center's Museum of Tolerance has adopted, linking the experience of Jews under the Nazis to a wider national and international context. It serves as a way of resonating with Jews and other ethnic groups who seek a specific cultural association along with a broader human connection.

Exhibiting Jews: Multiple Exemplars of Jewish Art

It would be impossible to write about American art in the 20th century without including Jewish artists whose work and identity as Jews were intertwined. In the first half of the 20th century, these included artists such as Ben Shahn, Abraham Rattner and Leonard Baskin, among others, all of whom used Jewish themes in some of their work. Often their art served as a social commentary, with the Judaism connected to ideas of social consciousness (Auerbach 341). The art was Jewish, albeit in a secular, political vein.

Max Weber's paintings and sculptures were different. He was, perhaps, the first major American artist to create a recognized body of work that could be identified as Jewish—both in Judaic and political terms (Baigell 341). Weber was born in Bialystock, Poland, in 1881. He traveled to New York when he was 10. During the first two decades of the 20th century, when Weber was in his 20s and 30s, he developed a reputation as a major American artist influenced by and following the path of the great French and German fauvists and cubists. However, shortly after the Russian

Revolution in 1918, he began a series of prints touching directly on Jewish subjects. In all, he completed more than 60 works with explicitly Jewish themes from 1920 to 1950 (Baigell 342). In November 2002, a major retrospective of Weber's work was exhibited in San Francisco.

Weber's works included portraits of rabbis and depictions of Jewish men poring over holy books, men talking or praying in synagogues and ceremonial objects. Weber, who died in 1961, attempted to connect viewers to a recollected Jewish and Yiddish past. Despite this reaching back to his origins, Weber, who considered himself an Orthodox Jew, adapted to modern American life. He was an assimilated modernist who kept kosher (Baigell 342) and responded directly against anti-Semitism through both political activism and painting (Baigell 347). But the images and Jewish themes in Weber's work do not portray Jewish life in America. They refer back to the early portraits of Jewish ghetto life that he encountered in his younger days as an immigrant living in a New York ghetto. "The people pray, study and fall back on their past in the old country. But they are also a people in the midst of joy, of religious (Hasidic) fervor" (Baigell 352).

While Weber was immersed in the art world, Arthur Szyk, more of a gifted illustrator and cartoonist than a painter or sculptor, spent much of his time deeply involved in political action. He used his art to raise political awareness in the United States, urging Americans to fight for Jewish survival and freedom. His voice was different from that of other Jewish American cartoonists and illustrators in the 1930s and 1940s, in large part because he was living in the midst of the European conflagration. Szyk was a Polish artist who had traveled throughout Poland in the 1930s and later, after the war started, served as a cultural ambassador at large in Switzerland and Great Britain for the Polish government. He believed his work should encompass the political and social issues of the day. At times he referred to his cartoons as "weapons of war," lampooning Nazi leaders and celebrating Allied soldiers (Goodwin 123-124).

Among Szyk's many illustrations were two that found themselves printed and reprinted throughout the Holocaust and years after: *Tel Hai* and *Tears of Rage*. Jewish organizations and publications seized upon them as a means of rallying the Jewish people. *Tel Hai,* created in 1936, depicted the story of Joseph Trumpeldor resisting the Arab attack on Tel Hai, a Jewish settlement in Palestine. Trumpeldor became a role model and a hero to succeeding generations of Jews. He stood for resistance rather than passive acceptance of fate. *Tel Hai* was subsequently reproduced many times in United States magazines and newspapers and served as "a valuable icon for American Jews" (Goodwin 126). In *Tears of Rage,* Szyk portrayed a young, Jewish soldier with an angry look on his face, a machine gun gripped in one hand and a slain patriarch clutching a torah scroll in the other. The word "stateless" was printed on the soldier's shoulder to call attention to the homelessness of the Jews. *Tears of Rage* was first drawn and shown in December 1942. Both of Szyk's famous illustrations became icons "of what a Jew should be and of what was necessary for Jewish survival in the modern world" (Goodwin 129).

Jewish Cartoonists

One way of describing Jewish American cartoonists is to characterize them as having grown more secure in expressing their Jewishness as the century moved forward. In the process, they also helped shape our popular culture. For entertainment, the East European masses in the first two decades of the 20th century turned to vaudeville, silent films and Yiddish theater— all facets of popular culture (of which cartoons and humorous illustrations were a representative form). The cartoons often began as satire, parody and jokes, but in the work of Jewish cartoonists, something else happened along the way. Ultimately, the cartoonists were men and women "in search of a predicament, a cause or a revelation" (Goodwin 169).

In the 1930s, for example, Superman began as a comic strip created by two commercial Jewish cartoonists, Joe Schuster and Jerry Siegel. However, the superhero soon became an American cultural touchstone. Over the next 70 years, the Superman figure found its way to theater, films, television and more recently, literary fiction. In 2000, Michael Chabon centered the world of comics and Superman in his novel *The Amazing Adventures of Kavalier and Klay*, in which two Jewish protagonists seize on the idea of creating a comic series, "The Escapist," to raise money for refugees and relatives in war-torn Europe.

Perhaps because of the popular appeal, museums and art galleries initially ignored cartoonists; the cartoonist's art, melding popular culture with commerce, was deemed by museum curators as well as by academic scholars as not serious enough to be exhibited (Goodwin 147). The list of Jewish cartoonists that fit this description includes Rube Lucius Goldberg, Albert Hirschfeld, Harvey Kurzman and Will Eisner. Goldberg (1883-1970) was one of the first Jewish American cartoonists; in the latter part of his career, his work mainly appeared on the editorial pages of newspapers. "At the height of his career, Goldberg was the most popular and best paid cartoonist in America," earning $125,000 in 1928 (Goodwin 149-150).

Hirschfeld, a gifted illustrator born in 1903, who only recently died at age 99 (in January 2003), had a retrospective show in New York as recently as 2000. His work has appeared in *The New York Times*, but he eventually bridged the twin worlds of journalism and art. Today, a Manhattan art gallery exhibits his work, and he has published several coffee-table books. A documentary film about him, *The Line King*, was nominated for an Academy Award in 1996. He is often linked with such famous book illustrators as Howard Pyle, N.C. Wyeth and Norman Rockwell (Goodwin 151).

Kurzman and Eisner used comic books as their medium for conveying statements about our American culture and about their own Jewish identity. Eisner, born in 1917, was one of the first cartoonists to deal with the complexity of functioning as a Jew in mid-century America. The city he depicted was a raw one, filled with violence and cruelty. Eventually, he expanded the scope of his work to produce something akin to a "graphic novel" (Goodwin154-157). Kurzman (1924-1993), meanwhile, was a mid-century popular culture junkie. He became a comic book fan as a child and was fascinated with all aspects of popular culture: comics, Hollywood, mainstream music, television, and perhaps most important of all, the effect the culture had on the urban young. In the early 1950s, his comics focused on war themes, but then he hit on the idea of spoofing popular culture in general, everything from television, films, media and the comic books themselves. He began to draw parodies that appeared in a newly formed, highly successful comic book, *Mad Magazine*. Many of the early issues of *Mad*, the brainchild of another Jewish illustrator, Al Feldstein, were the work of Kurzman. He was the smart, Jewish kid undercutting the social and media pretensions that surrounded Madison Avenue and the supposedly modern hip urbanites in New York. The trademark figure, Alfred E. Neuman, was a riff on the name of an eminent Hollywood composer Alfred Newman (Goodwin 157-160).

Two other cartoonists, Saul Steinberg and Art Spiegelman, belong to the second half of the 20th century, a period when Jews were not only defining popular culture but also losing their outsider status and gaining acceptance as full-fledged members within American society. The Romanian-born Steinberg (1914-1999) was perhaps best known for his drawings and covers (in excess of 600) which appeared in *The New Yorker*. He was educated as an architect in Italy and came to New York via Santa Domingo shortly after the war began. Compared to his fellow cartoonists, he was exceptionally well educated. Witty and quiet, he soon gained an appreciative following in New York's art circles. His *New Yorker* cover depicting New York City and outlying suburbs that stretched to the Pacific Ocean became an instant classic. In 1974, he was awarded the Medal for Graphic Art from the American Academy of Arts and Letters. New York's most prestigious art galleries represented him, and his work was shown at the Whitney Museum and the Museum of Modern Art (Goodwin 160-164).

Spiegelman, born in 1948, also drew covers and cartoons for *The New Yorker*. Spiegelman knew the Holocaust intimately because his father was a survivor. His two-volume masterwork, *Maus: A Survivor's Tale* (rejected by numerous publishers) and *Maus II* have received extraordinary critical and popular acclaim.

In 1992, Spiegelman received a Pulitzer Prize (Goodwin 164). On one level, it seems extraordinary to produce a Holocaust comic book. *Maus,* a story of the Holocaust, is part biography and autobiography, darting back and forth between Spiegelman (the boy) and his father (a survivor). Influenced by *Mad Magazine,* Spiegelman's cartoons turned personal and did not flinch from exposing the details of a life lived in pain, horror and confusion (Goodwin 166). In December 1991 and January 1992, New York's Museum of Modern Art exhibited all 269 pages of *Maus* along with studies, photos and tapes of Spiegelman's work, which became part and parcel of the new American culture. By century's end, a Jewish sensibility, and a Jewish subject, had become one of the defining elements of American popular culture (Goodwin 164-167).

Too Jewish?

If by the 1990s American Jews and the larger society could radically respond to a comic book about the Holocaust, it was only a slight stretch for them to accept the controversial art exhibit of 1996, *Too Jewish?*, which opened first in New York at the Jewish Museum. It seemed almost inevitable, as Carol Ockman, professor of art history at Williams College, wrote in the September 1996 volume of *Artforum International Magazine.* She observed that the variety of artworks in the *Too Jewish?* exhibit were produced primarily by secular, third- and fourth-generation American Jews and reflected their entry into the arena of identity politics (Ockman 3).

Ockman argues that "while Jews had been involved in the political activism of the 1960s, their economic status, their acceptance and readiness for assimilation, had kept them from being perceived as marginalized" in the way that, for example, African Americans were. *Too Jewish?* therefore, owes some "debt to feminist, race and queer studies." It is the confidence of acceptance and inclusion into the majority culture that has permitted the artists' freedom to mock and satirize the cliches of Jewish identity (Ockman 3).

Ockman sees the exhibition as connecting with people like

herself, "a Jew born after the Holocaust" who has attended shows that addressed "the history of the Jews, but not my history as a Jew" (Ockman 1). It is precisely the challenging exploration of the relationship between identity and Jewish stereotypes that she finds so appealing. The ability to engage Jewishness with humor and to reproduce cliches about Jewish women, faces and rituals seems to her to be an expression of Jewish wit and irreverence and embraces the identity itself. As she remarks, "it took courage to confront stereotypes at full tilt" (Ockman 2). Ultimately, Ockman admires artists and curators for inserting "Jewishness into a world that attempts to eradicate it" (Ockman 2).

Not everyone was quite so appreciative of the show. Daniel A. Segal, professor of world history and cultural anthropology at Pitzer College in Claremont, Calif., disliked the exhibit for perpetuating stereotypes that he found to be false and misleading (Segal 1-6). Specifically, he finds the visual stereotyping of Jewish noses and the acceptance of a particular form of feminine beauty in America (i.e. not Jewish) offensive as well as untrue. Segal's complaint is that *Too Jewish?* "produces and exhibits rather than challenges traditional identities" (Segal 5). Segal rejects the idea that the viewer presumably can tell that someone is Jewish just by physical appearance, by looking at the Barbra Streisand profiles, the Barbie dolls and the variety of Jewish noses. The show implies that the stereotypes of Jewish identity are all true, he says (Segal 4).

Haggada

It is of course possible for Jewish artists to deal with Jewish rituals and culture in new ways that are not satirical or even confrontational. Earlier this year, for example, the Reform movement introduced a new *Haggada,* or guide to the seder, called *The Open Door.* The title expresses a desire to be inclusive, to welcome everyone. This book, the first to appear since 1974 under the auspices of the Central Conference of American Rabbis, is the fifth version published by the Reform Movement (Elwell 1). It represents a first, a fully egalitarian *Haggada*, and in that sense is tied to the changing times for Jews in America (as is the publication and acceptance of Spiegelman's *Maus* and the *Too Jewish?* exhibition that toured America). *The Open Door* breaks new ground by being the first *Haggada* ever to present readers with the option "of reciting each prayer in Hebrew, using either masculine or feminine God language" (Elwell 1).

The 29 color drawings created for the *Haggada* are the work of Ruth Weisberg, an artist and dean of the School of Fine Arts at USC. She has turned to Jewish themes in much of her past work. Here her drawings "integrate images of modern-day Seder participants and the ancient Israelites living in Egypt." She includes an illustration that has never before appeared: a scene where the Israelites call to God—marking the "borderline between slavery and freedom" (Elwell 1).

One image has undergone a transformation in meaning. A soaring eagle serves as an allusion to a verse near the completion of the *Haggada* that reads: "Our arms spread like soaring eagles, our legs light as gazelles." But September 11, 2001, has given the image an added meaning, linking the freedom of early Israelites to that found in the United States today (Elwell 1).

Exhibiting Jews and Jewish Works in the 21st Century

Traditional American museums began to change in the latter part of the 20th century. They began to collect photography in a significant way, as can be seen today at the Getty Center in Los Angeles and the Museum of Modern Art in New York. They also started exhibiting "installations" that included videos as works of art, set aside space for conceptual pieces (and, in some instances, for performance art), and even began to award exhibitions to a few cartoonists at the Museum of Modern Art in New York. In this way, the meaning and role of a museum in its community has received, and continues to receive, challenges from a host of sources, many of them art historians and museum curators.

The changes have been particularly felt in the Jewish museum world. In part, that is a result of its smaller, more focused circle: a Jewish museum, with Jewish trustees and curators, and primarily a Jewish audience. But there are also expectations about Jewish identity in America, the history of the Jewish people, dealing with that awesome moment in the Jewish recent past, the Holocaust, and sorting out the highly focused audience. Is the Jewish museum aimed at Jews alone or Jews and those non-Jews who wish to learn about Judaism and/or ethnicity and identity? "Moreover, given those options, how sophisticated a museum does one need in order to compete? ...How does one stay alive [with] funding being a continual concern" (Freudenheim 86)?

The change in exhibit content was foreshadowed by the acclamation given to Art Spiegelman for his cartoon books, *Maus and Maus II,* which include depictions of the Holocaust and the world of survivors that were unthinkable less than a generation ago. That appeared to lay the groundwork for comic artist and illustrator Ben Katchor, who was recently awarded a major show at San Francisco's Magnes Museum (March 21-June 30, 2002). Katchor, 51, calls his drawings "picture stories." They resemble the comic strip of the 1930s but fall somewhere between "graphic novel, comic and cartoon" (Magnes Museum). What made them unusual, initially, was that they gathered a following in quite disparate places, including Yiddish newspapers and comic magazines, New York periodicals and, eventually, *The New York Times* (Magnes Museum).

His "picture stories" did not hesitate to trample on sensitive Jewish issues. There was a gritty New York feel to most of the stories, so they almost seemed like a cartoon version of cinema noir. But there were also bits of Yiddish culture in the stories, drawn from the earlier days of the 20th century. Mostly, though, Katchor's characters are recognizable as Jews: exiles and *émigrés* caught in a world where national and cultural identities are forced out into the open by the cartoonist (Magnes Museum). His reception suggests that the non-Jewish and Jewish communities are able to accept his blunt and "politically incorrect" view of Jews in America without necessarily endorsing it.

Two Museums

If "acceptable" content has begun to change within the Jewish museum world, so too have the museums themselves. Often, they emphasize multimedia representations of Jewish life and culture in America. There is technology galore, such as interactive computers, discovery kits for children and archaeology games that attempt to convert the museum observer into a participant.

The concept of converting the visitor from viewer to participant lies at the heart of some of the newer museums, such as the Museum of Jewish Heritage—A Living Memorial to the Holocaust. It opened its doors in New York City in September 1997. Situated in Battery Park, symbolically positioned opposite Ellis Island and the Statue of Liberty, its collection consists of more than 2,000 photographs, 24 documentary films and videos and 800 historical artifacts (Maiman 1-3). The intention is educational, and the museum's goal is to personalize the experience as much as possible. The effort is always to involve the observer with what is being observed (Maiman 1-3).

In addition to artifacts, there are videos, testimonials from director Steven Spielberg's Survivors of the Shoah Visual History Foundation and chronicles from eyewitnesses. For example, there is an exhibit that focuses on the German passenger ship St. Louis, which in 1939 carried mostly Jewish passengers seeking in vain to escape from Nazi Germany. As the ship reached first Cuba and then the Americas, the passengers were denied asylum and the ship was ultimately forced to return to Europe and the horrors of World War II. "Video is the primary documentary tool of the age," says David Altshuler, director of the museum (Maiman 2).

Altshular says his museum's name "expresses our function as a cultural and educational institution" (Maiman 2). As author William Maiman explains, the museum's environment, which at times is conceptualized like a theater set, "is designed not only to educate visitors about the Holocaust, but to place that event in the context of modern Jewish history, and to send a message of renewal" (Maiman 3).

By now, the Holocaust is familiar to anyone who watches films and television or who attends museums. Yet as one critic writing about the Holocaust in different art forms has observed, "one is struck again by how many ways the same narrative maintains its force." The critic also noted that the strength of the presentations of the Holocaust in a museum owe something to how personalized they are, often concentrating on "a single group of real people—individuals too often lost in the retelling of history" (Freudenheim 2). For example, photographs of Jewish children deported from France, combined with video testimonials from Spielberg's Survivors of the Shoah Visual History Foundation, impart a sense of immediacy to the viewer as well as a feeling of deep emotion.

However, for Tom Freudenheim, there is a problem in the museum's approach. He is struck "by the tension between addressing an audience of Jews who could learn more about their heritage and non-Jews, for whom the Jew is explained." And by extension, he faults the museum for emphasizing, somewhat boastfully, "all the important people in various fields of endeavor who happened to be Jewish" (Freudenheim "Museum..." 3).

The central conundrum for the Jewish Heritage Museum and other Jewish museums is that the critics raise a series of important questions that cannot be answered by their exhibits alone. According to Freudenheim, among the profound questions that museums face are: "Why have the Jewish people survived over the centuries? What constitutes the essence of Judaism today" (Freudenheim "Museum..." 3)? But the exhibitions at the Skirball Cultural Center, Jewish Heritage Museum, Jewish Museum of New York and others never actually provide anything approximating an answer. Instead, there are "confused messages of art/artifact constantly at war with the intellectual premise of the examination" (Freudenheim "Museum..." 3). In effect, objects of art and beauty are sometimes asked to serve a higher educational purpose, more than their weight or beauty can sustain.

Dealing With the Holocaust

If nothing else, the Holocaust has become part of popular culture. Steven Spielberg's *Schindler's List* and Roberto Benigni's *Life is Beautiful* were successful, Academy Award-winning films; in addition, two documentaries on the Holocaust were awarded Oscars in the 1990s. There was also *Maus,* which won the Pulitzer Prize, and the controversial book *Hitler's Willing Executioners,* by Daniel J. Goldhagen, which received extensive praise and coverage. Additionally, there has been great success for new museums devoted to the Holocaust in Washington, New York and Berlin. The Holocaust moreover has received more attention in the last decade, but in the process, it could be argued, it has ceased being the sole property of the Jews.

We have witnessed a rapid progression from popular culture dramatizing the Holocaust to the point where scholars are once again "assessing the Holocaust as a subject for representation" (Olin 463). A number of renowned scholars have addressed the subject, such as James Young in *Reading and Writing About the Holocaust*. Serious investigations by Lawrence Langer of survivor testimonies, along with studies by Saul Friedlander analyzing "the ways in which literature, film, art, memories and testimony have represented the Holocaust" have all raised questions about the Holocaust and the adequacy with which it has been dealt. It is Friedlander who has again echoed author Theodor Adorno, who wrote at war's end "to write poetry after Auschwitz is barbaric" (Olin 463-464).

This has made it simple for some critics. Visual representations of the Holocaust are faulted simply because, according to Margaret Olin, associate professor at the School of the Art Institute of Chicago, they violate the 2nd Commandment. The dictum is clear: It is not possible or permissible to beautify the historical nightmare. However, she notes that studies have demonstrated there is a large body of "visual representations" of the Holocaust, enough so that there now exists a "received" visual history. We can ignore it, but that will make neither the work nor the studies disappear or become insignificant (Olin 464).

According to Olin, the most authoritative study of the Holocaust is *Depiction and Interpretation: The Influence of the Holocaust on the Visual Arts*, a documentary created by Ziva Amishai-Maisels in 1992. Her work traces Holocaust imagery from its beginnings in the years before World War II to the present day. What she provides is an analysis of the ways different categories of artists dealt with the Holocaust. For example, the "Christian artists tended to focus on death, while the Jewish artists emphasized survival"(Olin 464). Amishai-Maisels also scrutinizes the use of barbed wire in drawings of the concentration camps. She notes that in their drawings, inmates "placed barbed wire behind inmates in their images, non-inmates… placed the barbed wire in front" (Olin 465). The effect of the inmates' placement of the barbed wire was to situate the observer inside the camp, while non-inmates' drawings positioned the viewer outside the camp so that the prisoners were entreating the viewer for help. Olin believes that when the viewer is seen as inside the camp, the inmate is "the subject of his own experience." Those that place the viewer outside the barbed wire "treat the inmate as an exotic other, the object of consumption and pity" (Olin 465).

Nevertheless, there are problems. "Amishai-Maisels' valuable study papers over a conceptual vacuum. It assumes the phenomenon that it should be investigating: the problematic nature of the representation of the Holocaust" (Olin 465). Moreover, sometimes she turns judgmental, reprimanding some abstract artists by asserting they are avoiding the issue, while simultaneously praising other abstract artists for resorting to abstraction as a way of coping with the Holocaust. The critic herself appears to have problems with unrecognized subjectivity (Olin 466).

Olin emphasizes that the danger in some of these studies is that the Holocaust may have become an archetype, even as we recognize that it was an experience for a specific individual. By generalizing and falling back on visual icons to depict the unspeakable, we may fall into the error of misrepresenting the individual's life story. If we are left with only individual accounts told visually, it becomes difficult to apply the experience to a broader historical meaning. On the other hand, there is the danger, Olin concludes, that the more the Holocaust takes on a historical perspective, the more it seems to fall outside history (Olin 467).

Ironically, another outcome of visually representing the Holocaust has been the so-called "Holocaust effect." This term, coined by Ernst Van Alphen in his book *Caught by History*, describes the effect of evoking Holocaust associations through the use of seemingly distant, but related artistic subject matter. For example, in 1987, the artist Christian Boltanski's installation of photographs of Jewish schoolchildren circa 1933 Vienna led to an unsurprising Holocaust association, because the work implies the children may have perished within the next decade. However, Boltanski's 1990 installation *Dead Swiss,* a compilation of photographs from recent obituaries, also appears to refer to the Holocaust when in fact the two are not related. In the hands of this artist, and in our own minds because of our popular culture experience with the Holocaust, death and destruction "have become emblems of the Holocaust," according to Olin (Olin 467).

In such exhibitions and many other forms, the Holocaust is evoked in disparate images that have little to do with the Holocaust itself. The experience, like the representation of old and new art, appears to change constantly. We must remember it, but we cannot hold fast to one fixed image, or one fixed moment, that represents the Holocaust.

Shows Go On

In this environment, current contemporary Jewish exhibits still continue. The Bowers Museum of Cultural Art in Santa Ana presented an exhibit in October 2001 titled *The Holy Land: David Roberts, Dead Sea Scrolls, House of David Inscription*, a show with nearly two dozen artifacts, primarily from the Israel Museum and the Israel Antiquities Authority (Bowers Museum Press Release). The Armand Hammer Museum, of course, has its own permanent collection. But like many other museums, it also mounts traveling exhibitions such as the *Too Jewish?* show, while the Skirball Cultural Center featured the recent travelling Freud exhibition.

A recent exhibition at Los Angeles' Autry Museum of Western Heritage, *Jewish Life in the American West*, was very much in line with the Casden Institute's mission, and afforded us the opportunity to explore the challenges of presenting Jewish American themes in 21st century museum exhibitions. In conjunction with the exhibit, programs were presented that integrated academics, performers and laypeople in a public discourse about the Westerners' backgrounds and how they involved the American Jewish community and its popular culture.

A panel discussion jointly organized by the Casden Institute and Autry Museum considered the issue of "Exhibiting Jews: History, Controversy and Concepts." Panelists included Nancy Berman, director emeritus and curator at large for the Skirball Cultural Center, John Gray, executive director and chief executive of the Autry Museum and Constance Wolf, director and chief executive of the Jewish Museum in San Francisco.

Conclusion

It is evident from our discussion in this chapter that Jews have played, and continue to play, an important role in the American art world as museum visitors, patrons, supporters, artists, scholars and critics. The intrinsic role of Jews in art is ironic considering the marginalization of Jewish art and artists in the 19th century and some of the 20th. Until fairly recently, Jewish art was ignored or avoided. Even upon its acceptance as a valid form of artistic expression, the definition of "Jewish art" eluded many scholars and critics for decades. Museums, as well, have suffered from an identity crisis about Jewishness and Jewish art: Should Jewish museums cater only to Jews, or should their goal be more universal, attempting to attract a wider audience by featuring both Jewish and non-Jewish artists and themes?

Controversy surrounds these issues, and it is clear that no simple answer exists. Is Jewish art comprised only of works by Jewish artists, or is it something that should consider the theme of the art more than the culture of the artist? For example, the *Too Jewish?* show attempted to illuminate the condition and place of Jews in American society today, but some critics believe it perpetuated false and misleading stereotypes. Is this, then, Jewish art? Museums, scholars and critics have debated this issue for years. The future of the Jewish art world is unknown, as it evolves with the prevailing cultural, political and aesthetic notions.

Central to this question of the definition of Jewish art is the heritage of the artist. Initially, Jewish art was seen as work created by Jewish artists. For a time, however, art history was viewed solely in terms of nationality, thus excluding Jewish artists from serious consideration (Soussloff 5). Bezalel Narkiss helped change this perspective by engaging in a massive study of art by Jews. Though he admits that no single style can be gleaned from this examination as Jewish artists were spread across centuries and around the world, he believes a common cultural heritage does exist (Rolnick 41). Presently, the culture of the artist is less important to Jewish art than the themes of the art itself. A Jewish artist can present non-Jewish art, and non-Jews are deemed capable of creating "Jewish" works. In this way, Jews can feel assured they won't be marginalized as "Jewish artists." However, at the same time, they have forfeited certain issues such as the Holocaust as their sole realm for artistic expression. While the Holocaust may no longer be the exclusive artistic property of Jews, this shift to include other artists may be a benefit, helping to ensure that a variety of experiences, from both a Jewish and non-Jewish perspective, will be presented.

At one time, Jewish art was nonexistent; Jews feared breaking the 2nd Commandment against idol worship (Rolnick 41). Consequently, Jewish art is a relatively young discipline. The questions surrounding the definition of Jewish works of art, in large part, stem from the newness of the art form, and the transient nature of this definition is understandable and, in fact, necessary. As time progresses and the cache of Jewish art increases, it is likely that an accepted definition will eventually be agreed upon.

The purpose of the artwork, as mentioned, has become central in determining whether it is Jewish or not. For example, *tikkun olam* (repairing the world) is a theme prevalent in much Jewish art. Based on the presence of this theme, art can be categorized as "Jewish" despite the culture or nationality of the artist. This Messianic view does not need to be a conscious act on the part of the artist; it simply needs to be present.

The questions surrounding Jewish art are not limited to artists alone, however. Scholars and critics have experienced similar struggles with their personal identities and professional obligations in terms of defining Jewish art. This tendency may have emerged, in part, from the history of American art criticism. As Soussloff notes, many influential founders of American art history since World War II fled here from Germany (1). Thus, the attempt by art historians to remove cultural considerations from their criticism may stem in part from the Nazi persecution of the Jews. As a subconscious attempt to minimize their outsider status, these *émigrés* may have downplayed and ignored their Jewish heritage as well as the Jewishness in the art they examined. Today, the attitude of art historians and scholars is almost diametrically opposed to this earlier approach, with many claiming that their own subjective cultural, religious and ethnic views must play a part in their criticism (Soussloff 1-12).

This view may have developed because of, or along with, a shift in American society as a whole. Embracing one's ethnicity and individuality has replaced the sense of universality and similarity in our culture. This change, perhaps, has helped to diminish the "insider/outsider" mentality that previously existed. Our society no longer espouses a single, central "insider." Instead, one is capable of fitting into a number of different, often culturally and ethnically-based, circles.

Museums have adapted to these changes in society as well. While some museums have tried going in new directions with familiar objects (National Foundation for Jewish Culture 1), others have vastly modified their approach to patrons. A common contemporary trend prizes multimedia presentations and interactive aspects of museum-going, involving the visitor as a participant as opposed to a strict observer. Jewish museums, despite the fact that they are a relatively new addition to the art world, are not immune from these changes in society. Like Jewish artists, who are no longer solely associated with "Jewish art," Jewish museums are no longer solely concerned with attracting Jews but often seek to appeal to a broader base of potential visitors. These museums were designed to take the message or theme of a work of art more heavily into account than the actual aesthetics, so that visitors would be able to explore meaningful issues (National Foundation for Jewish Culture 1). Originally, museums were wary of including "ethnic" exhibitions, fearing that these artists would, potentially, provide works of dubious artistic merit (Starger 3). It is apparent today that this is not the case, but nonetheless Jewish museums have shifted their focus, perhaps in part to offset their recent need to compete with cultural centers and museums for an audience. This shift by Jewish museums has served as an overt recognition that they are concerned with "culture" as a whole and not strictly Jewish culture. In some ways this could be seen as a reverse of the overall societal shift. While, ethnically, our country is separating into individuals, many museums, both Jewish and non-Jewish, are consolidating, including Jewish and non-Jewish exhibits.

In conclusion, Jews have had a profound impact on the history and current state of art in our society. This effect, though not limited to, has been most profound in its impact on "Jewish art," the definition of which has changed over the decades and has yet to be solidified. Jewish museums and art critics and scholars have faced similar struggles with their identity, and the latest trend seems to be to embrace Jewishness while acknowledging the validity of non-Jewish art and artists. It is important to remember that Jewish art is, in part, so difficult to define because it is a comparatively young discipline. Furthermore, one should consider whether or not a cohesive definition of Jewish art is necessary; perhaps, like the artwork itself, asking the question forces the interpreter to seek his or her own answer; that would seem to be what is most important.

Chapter Five

CULTURE:
Jewish Contributions to American Film

In the past 100 years, American films have played a dominant role not only in shaping the cultural life of the United States, but also in generating the images and dreams that define who we are as a nation and how we are supposed to live. That these prescriptions for living an idealized, American life were influenced by a group of Jewish immigrants from Eastern Europe seems ironic and remarkable. This chapter recounts the story of how these men established the film industry and found themselves ruling "an empire" of their own making.

Initially, the men who became moguls in Hollywood organized storefront theaters in New York City, largely for a market of fellow immigrants, which quickly expanded into an American mass market audience. Nickelodeon storefronts soon turned into local movie theaters and in some instances grand movie "palaces." The film center shifted from New York to Hollywood, and the immigrant Jewish salesmen and entrepreneurs who distributed and exhibited these new movies became Jewish moguls running multimillion-dollar movie studios, with stars, national distribution systems and a vast publicity mill designed to promote and protect their empire (Gabler "An Empire…" 1-7). As Neal Gabler, senior fellow at USC's Lear Center, has written in his book, *An Empire of Their Own*: "Ultimately, American values came to be *defined* largely by the movies the Jews made. Ultimately, by creating their idealized America on the screen, the Jews reinvented the country in the image of their fiction" (Gabler "An Empire…" 7).

In this chapter, we will discuss the background of the Jewish moguls who established the movie business, the changes that occurred in their lifestyles as they rapidly gained immense wealth, power and fame, and the effect the newfound prominence had on their sense of identity as Jews. They were a self-conscious, ambitious minority who unexpectedly had acquired enormous influence while living in the glare of a national spotlight. They wished for nothing so much as to be accepted by the Gentile establishment, who represented for them the America to which they longed to belong. We also will examine their vision of America, and how this was translated into stories that, in the beginning, emphasized the shedding of traditional values and religious separateness while encouraging assimilation.

Jewish characters and stereotypes were present in their early silent films. However, as the film industry began to dominate the American popular culture scene and gain a wider middle-class audience, the Jewish moguls became more circumspect. We will look at the fear of anti-Semitism and the insecurity of being labeled Jewish, which plagued these men, and see how that resulted in the virtual elimination of all traces of Jews and Judaism on the screen.

We also have selected several Jewish filmmakers and will study the effects of their work on the American audience, searching for a particular way to define what makes a film Jewish. We will attempt as well to review some contemporary trends in American Jewish filmmaking, from efforts to create "fictional" portraits of the Holocaust to new films about subjects that are outside mainstream American life, such as the gay and lesbian world, Orthodox Jewry and certain autobiographical documentaries. We will point out some of the radical changes in films that followed in the second half of the 20th century as the Jewish moguls faded from the scene and the Hollywood studio system came to an end. It is not a minor coincidence that during this period, the lives of American Jews changed almost as dramatically as the stories being depicted on the television and movie screens.

We have relied throughout this chapter on a variety of sources: scholarly works by academics; essays by critics and scholars in film journals; and news accounts in general-interest magazines and Jewish periodicals. To varying degrees, many of these sources emphasize the ways in which, to use Gabler's phrase, the Hollywood Jews "colonized the American imagination." (Gabler "An Empire…" 7). In the process, the Jewish immigrants who rapidly became Jewish moguls tried to avoid in their own lives, and the lives of the characters in their films, any Jewish characteristics. It is one of the ironies reflected in this chapter that they came to believe in the imaginary America they had invented, and in its imagined code of values. These beliefs could not be sustained in the face of such horrors as the Holocaust and such triumphs as the successful integration of Jews in American life.

The Immigrant Generation

Stephen J. Whitfield, professor of American studies at Brandeis University, has written that Jewish Americans have contributed somewhat disproportionately to the nation's cultural life (Whitfield XI-XVI.). Whitfield was a keynote speaker at the 2002 "In Search of American Jewish Culture: Competing Currents" event co-sponsored by the Casden Institute for the Study of the Jewish Role in American Life and Hebrew Union College-Jewish Institute of Religion. American films were the primary example of such disproportionate cultural contributions. Jewish immigrants, primarily from Eastern Europe, were the distributors, exhibitors, and marketing and sales strategists who launched the film industry.

They rented the nickelodeons and distributed the motion picture reels for the flood of immigrants who had come to the United States in search of opportunity and a better life. Their efforts were wildly successful and soon they became producers, heads of film studios and some of the wealthiest men in America (Gabler "An Empire..." 11-183).

After two decades, these successful movie industry professionals began to search for respectability and inclusion in America, which seemed to them to require shedding the ethnicity that had first connected them to their mass audience—immigrants like themselves. They were encouraged in this partly out of fear of anti-Semitism and partly because of charges by people like industrialist Henry Ford, who said they were imposing Jewish propaganda on an unsuspecting American public. The Hollywood empire they had built changed the *idea* of America for Jews and Gentiles alike. The irony, as Gabler wrote, is that so much of modern America's images of itself were shaped by these Jewish film moguls, when all they actually set out to do was market entertainment for the immigrants, who became the nation's first mass cultural audience (Gabler "An Empire..." 7).

That mass American audience dates to the latter part of the 19th century. From 1877 to 1927, the number of Jews in the United States jumped from a mere 229,000 to 4,228,000 (Erens "The Jew..." 3). Jews still comprised a modest three-plus percent of the nation's population, but they were now a recognizable minority. This great wave of immigrants differed from previous Jewish settlers. The first early group had consisted largely of Sephardic Jews who migrated in the 17th and 18th century. Some were cultured professionals, others merchants and skilled workers (Erens "The Jew..." 3). Their numbers were small and they found it simple enough to filter into the social networks of the 13 colonies. The second wave, still modest in number, was a cohesive group, mainly from Germany—again, with education, skills and a Western orientation. They soon established themselves as bankers and merchants and skilled tradesmen (Erens "The Jew..." 3).

It was the third wave—the Jews who traveled to the United

States from Russia and Poland and other Eastern European countries in vast numbers from 1880 to 1924—who carried the seeds of great change. Almost 25 percent were illiterate. The majority had lived in segregated *shtetls*, dealt with government-fueled persecution and had faced rejection and violence from non-Jewish countrymen. They had adhered to their religious traditions and obeyed an autocratic village system that governed their lives (Erens "The Jew..." 3). In the United States, the government did not persecute them; but they encountered anti-Semitism from non-Jews and scorn and rejection from the German and Sephardic Jewish Americans who were ashamed to be linked with them. In 1881, for example, an article in a Jewish newspaper urged American Jews to visit Russia, before the next wave of immigrants arrived, and help Westernize them, so they would be less of an embarrassment (Erens "The Jew..." 3).

This combination of closed doors and rejection, accompanied by freedom of mobility and the right to pursue economic goals, provided the challenge and the opportunity for the men who founded the movie industry. Adolph Zukor's family history was typical. He came from a small Hungarian village. His father had died while he was an infant and his mother a few years later; he was raised by a steely uncle. Lonely, independent and unloved, Zukor made the journey to America to establish a new life and cut his ties to the past. There was nothing to which he could return (Gabler "An Empire..." 3). There was also Louis B. Mayer, who claimed that he forgot where in Russia he had been born and on what day. Years later, he appropriated July 4 for his birthday. He settled in Canada with his parents and learned to cope with an authoritarian and failed father. He left for Boston as a young man to try his hand at business. Another Hungarian, William Fox, was born in America to *émigrés* parents. His father was irresponsible, an immigrant failure, and Fox was forced at an early age to support his family and himself, "hawking soda pop sandwiches, and chimney black" (Gabler "An Empire..." 3).

The pattern in most cases was similar for the future Hollywood moguls. They rejected a past that had offered them little, and they struggled desperately to assimilate, to become a part of an

America that seemed to treat them as outsiders. They appeared often to come from families in which the father had died or had failed in his efforts to settle in the new land (Gabler "An Empire..." 4).

They found themselves locked out of the world they wished to enter and locked out of business enterprises that were already dominated by Gentile corporate leaders and upper-middle-class German Jews (Gabler "An Empire..." 5). However, the new nickelodeons—spun off from Thomas Edison's invention and seemingly aimed in a scattered fashion at the new immigrant population—were wide open as enterprises. There were no social barriers and no hierarchy of either Jewish or Gentile business interests blocking the way. No one had seen how to market this new form of mass culture. Entertainment, which at that time included vaudeville and theaters aimed at the middle classes, was controlled by the German Jews. But the new Jewish entrepreneurs—Louis B. Mayer, Samuel Goldwyn, William Fox and Adolph Zukor, among others—began to "rent cheap storefronts in immigrant neighborhoods, charging a nickel admission to the movies" (Friedman "The Jewish Image..." 11). Nickelodeons were not respectable, but they also were not costly and so within economic reach; it took only $400 to open a storefront theater (Gabler "An Empire..." 5).

The early moviegoer audience consisted largely of working-class immigrants, and the films that flickered on the screen reflected their interests and tastes. They focused on the immigrant's world, with reels that often were bawdy, comic and melodramatic; underneath the surface, the films also "emphasized the shedding of traditional and constricted religious and cultural patterns" (Quart 8) and told stories about clashes between the generations, coupled with efforts to assimilate. Later, the moving pictures broadened in plot and outlook, reflecting a more "American milieu characterized by intermarriage, economic achievement, mobility, freedom, and a general accommodation to American values" (Quart 8). America, meanwhile, was rapidly becoming an urbanized society, and many of the films reflected what was very much a Jewish experience. For example, intermarriage was one goal, and as one critic explained, the path for a Jew to become an American was by way of marrying an Irish girl (Friedman "The Conversion..." 45). The films championed plots that supported the idea of being American, middle class and upwardly mobile. It is these stories almost without exception that are chronicled in the first three decades of film (Erens "The Jew..." 4-5, 21). This also followed the path the Jewish immigrants pursued.

By the end of World War I, the Jewish moguls who controlled the new movie enterprise had begun to attract a much larger audience—namely, the Gentile and Jewish middle-class (Clarens 35). What the new audience wanted were cleaner and more respectable theaters and a product that spoke to their middle-class identity (Holberg 2). Jewish characters in films changed from "being objects of charity to providers of it," a recognition of the financial success of the Jews who controlled the new industry and their friends (Friedman "The Jewish Image..." 12). Fewer immigrant characters appeared on screen. According to critic Carlos Clarens, writing in *Film Comment*, it was not an artistic decision, because the Jewish moguls were from the outset businessmen, not intellectuals or artists or ideologues. They were not concerned about changing America, or the cinema as an art form, only about turning out a product that people would buy (Clarens 36). They enjoyed one large advantage over the Gentile and German Jewish entrepreneurs who were already established, and who had underestimated the market potential of this new form of entertainment: They were working-class immigrants and, as shrewd salesmen, responded to an audience they knew well. Their advantage, according to Gabler, was that "they understood public taste and were masters at gauging market swings, at merchandising, at pirating away customers and beating the competition." Perhaps most important of all, "as immigrants themselves, they had a peculiar sensitivity to the dreams and aspirations of other immigrant and working-class families" (Gabler "An Empire..." 5).

As their financial success increased dramatically in the 1920s, the film entrepreneurs began to long for inclusion in society, for the status that they believed their affluence should confer. Their motion pictures became, for them, the vehicles from which they might make the journey from outsiders to the very center of American life. They set about creating, in the studio system with its stars and the films they produced, a portrait of a new invented country. This new land featured ideals and myths—"an empire of their own, so to speak"—and was one in which "they would not only be admitted, but would govern as well" (Gabler "An Empire…" 5-6). In this America, fathers did not fail, families were warm and loving, and people (except for the villains) were decent and appealing and kind. In this new, imagined America, there were rarely any Jews, despite the Jewish control of the film industry. The images and the stories were so compelling that the Jewish moguls and the mass audience of moviegoers came to believe in these American portraits and myths. Some critics contend that, beyond anything else, this may have been the Jewish moguls' "most enduring legacy." (Gabler "An Empire…" 6).

Visions of America

The early films—social comedies and melodramas, produced quickly and cheaply—had been free of myths about America. Film critics and scholars have offered persuasive evidence to demonstrate that these films—short, broad, pulp stories and extended visual jokes about the immigrant's world—were filled with depictions of Jews and Jewish life. They presented a Jewish immigrant's vision of America, albeit one in which assimilation often was the norm, and in which Jews and Gentiles were, or would be, indistinguishable from one another (Quart 8). Patricia Erens, professor of communication at Rosary College in River Forest, Ill., points out in *The Jew in American Cinema* the ways in which the early nickelodeon films resembled the stories the Jewish film entrepreneurs knew from their own lives, and the lives of parents, family and friends. The plots were filled with "tales of pogroms, immigration, ghetto living, and of upward mobility" (Erens 4).

Critic Lester Friedman, meanwhile, has compiled a list of titles for "*Film Comment*," which illustrates that from 1900 to

1929, Jews figured in approximately 230 films (Friedman "The Conversion..." 40). Most important, they preceded the rise of Jewish production heads. Jewish stereotypes were therefore fair game, though only to a limited extent, because the exhibitors and distributors were Jewish and served as informal watchdogs, guarding against too negative a Jewish movie portrait. There were, for example, few if any Jewish gangsters or hustlers, even in the first several decades of silent films (Erens "The Jew..." 19).

Nevertheless, several negative stereotypes did appear: "the Scheming Merchant, the Old Parasite with lowered social status and the Comic Jew.... The emphasis on money is inescapable" (Erens "The Jew..." 19). These negative portraits of Jews, however, were limited. The Jewish agencies as well as the men inside the new film industry were concerned about the possibility of harm, either in the form of anti-Semitism or commercial ruin that might follow from such projections. The "Jewish Agitator," a figure who appeared in proletarian fiction in the 1930s, was also kept off the screen, as were adaptations of contemporary novels with strong Jewish characters. The potential rise of anti-Semitism was too threatening (Erens "The Jew..." 19).

The men who dominated the film industry in these early days, while sensitive to anti-Semitic outbursts, were unaware of how influential and important a product they controlled. Their silent films were simply short, quick amusements pitched at immigrants. They relied on a limited number of basic plots, such as poverty destroys character, poverty reveals character, and character helps one escape from the ghetto (Friedman "The Conversion..." 46). Any immigrant presumably could identify with Jews in these short reels and could see and laugh at his own prejudices (Friedman "The Conversion..." 48). The silent films functioned, in this sense, as a rite of passage that occurred on the screen. Critics, putting the best spin on the message, explained in later years that silent films supported the prevailing melting pot ideology, which assumed all immigrants would be assimilated as they were stirred into the American system. These were not meant to be documentary or informational films, but served nevertheless as a crude form of propaganda, leaving many American immigrants and American born viewers less nervous about Jews (Friedman "The Conversion…" 48).

In the last several decades, critics have singled out other patterns and stereotypes that the films of the early period embraced. Until the beginning of World War II, African-Americans were cast in silent and talking films "that reveled in racial types and flavors" (Clarens 35)—they often were depicted as lazy or simple or untrustworthy. Black images in films throughout the century were "variations on a limited number of character types, updated, redressed, but basically unchanged" (Erens "The Jew…" 25). Women particularly were stereotyped— they were seen more often than not as sentimental, dependent and weak, cast as " Victorian child/women, flappers, vamps, platinum blondes, Rosie-the Riveters, bobbysoxers, mammary goddesses and popcorn Venuses" (Erens "The Jew…" 26). They also were presented as overbearing Jewish mothers (Samberg 63). The Jewish mother image notwithstanding, Jewish characters were the one exception to the negative stereotyping, according to most critics. The film studios were scrupulous about keeping Jews portrayed in an unflattering light off the screen. (Erens "The Jew…" 19). Budd Schulberg's novel *What Makes Sammy Run,* optioned several times but never produced, featured a hustling, dislikable, untrustworthy Jew that was always deemed unsuitable or too unflattering to Jews. One producer suggested Sammy Glick, "the conniving Jewish protagonist" of the novel, "be changed to someone of indeterminate ancestry" (Gabler 304).

Scholars also have noted that early silent films occasionally had a Yiddish cultural undercurrent (Holberg 4). The immigrant's experiences furnished the narrative for these silent films, which were filled with references to pogroms, immigration and ghetto living; the happy ending was linked to upward mobility and assimilation (Erens "The Jew…" 4). These stories, featuring Jewish immigrants, were movies with which all immigrants could identify (Erens "The Jew…" 411).

They all seemed to come together in the acme of the Jewish immigrant film, *The Jazz Singer*, which was produced as the first "talking" motion picture in 1927. The audience—by this time middle class and, in many cases, a generation away from immigrant status—could see the talented Jewish singer turn away from family, tradition and religion to adapt to the new, modern America. Despite the use of sound and music for the first time, *The Jazz Singer* was a throwback, recapitulating the themes of the silent films aimed at the first generation of immigrants: success in America came about only through a rejection of religion and Jewish tradition, while acceptance required an accommodation to secularism. The American vision was clear, regardless of ethnic background: Assimilation was the desired goal (Friedman "The Conversion…" 48).

There was a time, earlier in the history of the film industry's development, when American motion pictures might have turned in a different direction, leaching power from the Jewish moguls and distributing the control and influence of our national culture among working-class groups and "worker filmmakers" (Ross XV). Steven J. Ross, professor of history at USC, has written about an often ignored part of silent film's early history, when motion pictures were created by groups outside the control of Jewish moguls in New York and Hollywood. Ross notes that because one-reelers in the early days were so inexpensive, working-class groups were able to produce movies that mirrored their experiences in the United States. These silent films were filled with stories about the class struggle (Ross 5) and were highly partisan, furthering a national dialogue "over values and the direction of American society" (Ross 6).

The films had their greatest currency when the mass audience itself consisted of working-class immigrants. Ross points out that by 1911, one-third of the population went to the movies; by 1920, with the audience expanding into the middle class, that number had jumped to nearly one-half of the American population (Ross 7). According to Ross, everyone from the American Federation of Labor to the Ford Motor Company to the Women's Political Union produced some of these films (Ross 7). They were an excellent vehicle for promoting dialogue and educating the new immigrants. Moreover, they had an impact. Connecticut mill workers in 1916 decided to strike after watching *The Blacklist*, while *The Jungle* in 1914, based on the novel by Upton Sinclair, influenced people to join the Socialist Party. The class-struggle implications of the films so alarmed government leaders that local and state censors began to ban worker films (Ross 8-9).

By the 1920s, moreover, Hollywood had come into existence. Films were now produced on the West Coast by studios that also controlled their distribution and exhibition. The film studios had become part of big business, and their owners were now mainstream capitalists, despite their East European Jewish background and their immigrant origins. Producing movies had become expensive—or at least more expensive—and the audience had expanded beyond the working class. Hollywood's executives "pushed the politics of American cinema in increasingly noncontroversial and anti-radical directions as films became a part of 'respectable' entertainment that catered to the rapidly expanding and amorphous ranks of the middle class" (Ross 9). Issues of social class were swept from the screen. As Ross sees it, the story was "one of the greatest power struggles in American history" (Ross 10) with the working class—and by implication, America—on the losing end of the conflict.

Solidly in control, as entertainment became a multimillion-dollar consumer product, the men who ran the film industry began their rapid climb toward great wealth. The acquisition of that wealth, and the influence over what became known as the "dream factory" of America, produced a marked change in the Hollywood moguls. Scholars have written that they tried to shed their identification with Jews and Jewishness in their films and their personal affairs (Quart 8). Deception had become part of their life, and their life itself became an exercise in deception (Saposnik "Jolson..." 410). They steered away from films that had Jewish subjects and forced their Jewish movie actors to change their names, so that Pauline Marion Levy became Paulette Goddard and Jacob Julius Garfinkle was turned into John Garfield. In 1937, Warner Bros. produced a film about the Dreyfus case, the story of a Jewish captain in the French army who was falsely accused and convicted of treason, called *The Life of Emile Zola* and never once mentioned the word Jew (Quart 8-9).

The moguls, who reputedly had little interest in Judaism, sought also to blend in as Americans and to reinvent themselves, in some cases dropping their Jewish wives (Saposnik "Jolson..." 411). Samuel Goldwyn divorced his Jewish wife and married a socialite actress, Frances Howard; Joseph Schenck who with Louis B. Mayer controlled MGM, married one of his movie stars, Norma Talmadge (Clarens 35). Jack L. Warner (born John Eichelbaum) of Warner Brothers and Harry Cohn, who ran Columbia Pictures, also divorced their Jewish wives, remarrying Gentile women and raising their children as Gentiles, hoping to gain them admission to restricted schools and clubs (Quart 35).

According to Gabler, the moguls bought mansions or had new ones built, acquired horses, took up riding and began to copy the manners, dress and hobbies of the wealthy Gentiles. It made little difference: They were still viewed as parvenu or upstarts, Jewish immigrants, rich but vulgar (Gabler "An Empire..." 2), even as they tried constantly to distance themselves from anything identified as Jewish. Gabler tells the story of writer Ben Hecht soliciting funds for Israel from director-producer David O. Selznick, and being turned down because Selznick claimed he was an American, not Jewish. Hecht, knowing that Selznick was a compulsive gambler, bet that if any three people Selznick named agreed he was an American and not a Jew, Hecht would admit defeat. The three men who had been selected ruminated for a moment and then said that of course Selznick was Jewish (Gabler 220-221). In fact, the longings never wholly disappeared, and the fear that they would never be fully accepted as Americans at times became the subtext of some of the films produced by the Jewish moguls (Saposnik "Jolson..." 423-424). Their background at times also affected their decisions, such as the time an adolescent Judy Garland, auditioning for Mayer, was coached to sing *Eyli, Eyli*, a song she had learned for a B'nai B'rith benefit. Mayer was moved to tears and signed her to an MGM contract (Saposnik "Jolson..." 417).

Occasionally, films managed to slip through the cracks in the system and focus on themes that suggested class conflict: Warner Bros.' *Dead End* in 1937; United Artists' *Modern Times* with

Charlie Chaplin in 1936; and 20th Century Fox's *Grapes of Wrath* in 1940. These were all exceptions to Hollywood's norm. As Steven J. Ross contends, even here "these productions empathized with the plight of individuals," not with class conflict and political ideology (Ross 244).

Hollywood was generally careful from 1930 to the start of World War II to keep Jewish characters off the screen. It was only after the war in 1947 that Fox produced *Gentleman's Agreement*, a film about anti-Semitism, in which the character played by Gregory Peck is not really a Jew, but a journalist passing as a Jew to write an exposé (Gabler 349). The producer of the film was Darryl F. Zanuck, and the director, Elia Kazan. Neither was Jewish. Only after the breakup of the studio system, the advent of television and the end of the Jewish moguls' rule were Jewish actors able to retain their own names. Jewish characters began to appear in films whose themes might be identified as Jewish. The screen adaptation of Leon Uris' novel *Exodus* in 1960 became a great success, making it easier for films such as *Yentl, Norma Rae, Hester Street* and *The Chosen* to be produced, despite their Jewish characters and themes.

Critics and Anti-Semites

The moguls in Hollywood were anxious about anti-Semitism, particularly when they thought it might undercut profits and/or jeopardize their control of the film industry. Feelings against Jews had increased with the surge in Jewish immigration in the latter 19th and early 20th centuries. Harvard and other elite universities instituted quotas to keep Jewish students to a restricted low number; the legal and medical professions were quick to segregate Jews and non-Jews; and anti-Semites such as industrialist Henry Ford protested Jewish control of the film industry. Ford used his *Dearborn Independent* newspaper for his attacks, referring to the Jewish producers as being "different from the prevailing standards of the American people" (Gabler "The Jewish Problem" 38). The Jewish studio heads responded by trying to be above reproach. Movies that became classics championed assimilation (Gabler "An Empire..." 2); the prevailing view was that drawing attention to ethnic roots might fracture American society. Filmmakers were alerted: putting forth any sort of cultural or political identity other than "American" was divisive and undesirable and might eventually result in indirect pressure from anti-Semites, lobby groups, even the government (Gabler "The Jewish Problem" 38). Late in 1940, for example, Joseph P. Kennedy, then the United States ambassador to Great Britain, urged the chief executives of Hollywood "to stop making anti-Nazi pictures or using the film medium to promote or show sympathy to the cause of the democracies versus the dictators." The Jews were being "blamed for the war," he told them, and "anti-Semitism was growing in Britain" (Gabler "An Empire..." 344).

Kennedy's view reinforced attitudes that were prevalent among Jewish organizations such as the American Jewish Committee and the Anti-Defamation League. They were cautious about any action that might be seen as increasing anti-Semitism. They urged Hollywood's leaders to soft-pedal anti-Nazi films and avoid linking Jews with radical politics, arguing that these political messages were best put forward by non-Jews (Herman 2). Their efforts, while successful with the Jewish film leaders, made little difference: Nothing would satisfy the anti-Semites, evangelical groups and congressmen, who resented the fact that Jews dominated the motion picture industry. The evangelists wanted films liberated from "the hands of the devil and 500 un-Christian Jews" and the Catholic Legion of Decency was concerned that Jews in Hollywood were "outside the moral sphere of American culture" and yet controlled the images and messages that were beguiling Americans (Gabler "An Empire..." 2). Red-baiters in Congress, meanwhile, saw Judaism as only a thinly disguised cover for communism, with movies "their chief form of propaganda" (Gabler "An Empire..." 2).

In Hollywood itself, there were complaints about Jewish control. The novelist Theodore Dreiser had fought over the scuttling of his masterpiece *An American Tragedy* by Paramount. "The movies are solidly Jewish.... The dollar sign is the guide.... That America should be led—the mass—by their direction is beyond all believing," he wrote to a friend (Gabler "The Jewish Problem" 38). Director Howard Hawks observed bitingly that the Jews in the studios were loud (Gabler "The Jewish Problem" 38), and F. Scott Fitzgerald described Hollywood as "a Jewish holiday, a gentiles [sic] tragedy" (Gabler "An Empire..." 2). Gabler notes that "Jews became the phantoms of the film industry they had created, haunting it but never able to inhabit it." They were accused of "conspiring against traditional American values," even as they embraced those values and sought desperately to be accepted as part of the conservative, governing power structure (Gabler "An Empire..." 2).

Attacks today are less frequent, perhaps because the studio system is long since dead and Jews have integrated into the American political and social system. Hollywood's power brokers today are producers, directors, actors and major film companies; many of these figures are Jewish. However, critic and scholar William E. H. Meyer Jr. wrote in *Literature-Film Quarterly* in October 1999 that little in "Jewish Hollywood" has changed. Meyer writes that far from keeping Jews off the screen, however, the new producers, directors and writers engage overtly in philo-Semitic propaganda. Jews are everywhere in today's films, he argues, inserted willfully as characters, and exercising a role as moral and sagacious advisers for no reason other than Jewish propaganda (Meyer Jr. 271-281).

Meyers' contention is that minor characters who are given a Jewish identity assume a moral weight in the films when the plot itself does not call for a specific ethnic background. This has occurred, according to Meyer, following the decline of the studio system. Where the older Jewish moguls were self-conscious and uncomfortable with a Jewish image and tried to keep their films American and without Jewish characters, the new directors, actors, producers and writers have no such discomfort. He cites a variety of films, including Kevin Pollack portraying Tom Cruise's friend Lt. Sam Weinberg in *A Few Good Men*, reminding Cruise's character that the army cannot tolerate bullies who beat a weaker kid (Meyer Jr. 273). The Jewish character's role, according to Meyer, is to appear sympathetic to the underdog hero (Cruise) and command him to pursue goals of social justice. Meyer asserts that the director, the producer and the writer of the film were all Jewish and implies that is why the superior ethics are extended to a Jewish character (Meyer Jr. 273).

Meyer contends that Jews will always be separate and different in their narrative history and in their aesthetic view from the rest of America, and true Americans must guard against them (Meyer Jr. 279-281). One notable change between past and present is that Meyer's essay, published three years ago, was accompanied by a footnote telling the reader that the article was deemed controversial and the editorial board held strong reservations about it and felt the need to follow up with a "reply" (Meyer Jr. 281).

Jewish Filmmakers

What determines whether a movie is Jewish? Ultimately, personal taste plays "an inestimable role," according to Kathryn Bernheimer in her introduction to *The 50 Greatest Jewish Movies* (Friedman "Hollywood's Image…" X). Stephen J. Whitfield, writing about the arts in general, acknowledges that it is difficult to locate "what is Jewish in American Jewish culture" (Whitfield 30).

In this section, forewarned by these scholars and critics, we have selected a number of Jewish filmmakers—the Fleischer brothers, Woody Allen, Mel Brooks and Steven Spielberg—who in their films have reflected back to us the role Jews have played in creating American film culture. The governing principle in our choice has been the filmmaker's Jewish identity, and the way in which, through his work, that identity has imprinted itself on all Americans.

The Fleischer Brothers

The Fleischer brothers, Max and Dave, belonged to the generation of Jews who followed Mayer, Zukor and Goldwyn. They grew up on the Lower East Side of New York at the turn of the century, children of immigrants. Their story could have been told in one of the silent movies of the day. They rebelled against parents and quit school, turning to drawing and animation and technical invention. They found fame and fortune as animators, for a brief while. By 1940, they had moved their animation studio from New York to Florida, their major cartoon, Betty Boop, had been severely cut down by the film industry's Hays Code, and they had lost the animation market to Walt Disney, a much more American competitor (Holberg 1-13). Today, they are a minor reference in the larger story of Hollywood and the Jews.

Unlike Mayer, Goldwyn and the other Jewish film moguls, the Fleischer brothers never tried to cut themselves off from their Jewish origins. Their taste and sensibility were always connected to the early immigrant experiences of New York's Lower East Side and never changed. Their animated films were filled with some of the bawdy and cartoon content of the early silent films that had played in the nickelodeon storefronts they frequented as children. By the 1930s, they had created their most popular animated sound film star, Betty Boop (Holberg 1). Some of their animated stories were violent and others played out the fantasy images of the immigrant desperately striving for assimilation. Their work featured a popular, almost vulgar tone that was a throwback to the sexual innuendo of the early silent films which had drawn the working-class immigrants to the nickelodeons (Holberg 3).

The Fleischer brothers also pitched their cartoons toward a specialized Yiddish-speaking audience, much in the way that the *Forward* newspaper still appealed to a special audience based in New York. There were Yiddish symbols and jokes, and the animated cartoons carried their "'more or less camouflaged' ...Yiddish-American background" (Holberg 6). Eventually, they expanded their cartoon film franchise to include Popeye the Sailorman and Superman, with the intent of attracting a wider American audience while holding on to the earlier Jewish immigrants. The Fleischers' animations, products of their Yiddish-American background, essentially "reflected the seduction and fears of assimilation for the 20th century Jew in a peculiarly American way" (Holberg 6-7). Jews had the freedom to choose whether to hold onto ethnicity, to be Jewish in America or simply meld into the wider society (Holberg 6-7).

Critic Amelia S. Holberg points out in *American Jewish*

History in December 1999 that while the Fleischer's insider appeal to the Yiddish-speaking immigrants was much appreciated, that same quality "marked their films as not quite ready for America's mass audience" (Holberg 8). Their inability to shed ethnicity, as had MGM, Paramount and Warner Brothers, caused the Fleischer brothers to lose in their competition with Disney. They were still locked in the past—their stories went off on a different line, sometimes emphasizing the immigrant as The Other in a raucous way, highlighting the cost and impossibility of shedding one's Jewish immigrant status to assimilate and be accepted by white America (Holberg 8).

They also came smack up against the new Hollywood code, addressed to a perceived middle-class set of standards. Betty Boop was too sexual, too provocative, the Hays censorship office declared in 1934. By 1938, she was off the screen (Holberg 1). Their animated films, meanwhile, "drew shock and laughs from precisely the material the nickelodeons had sought to exclude …15 years earlier." (Holberg 6). This occurred just as the major studios were carefully keeping negative Jewish images off the screen and acting as though the United States was free of Jews. Although the moguls assumed that assimilation was what all Americans wanted, the Fleischer brothers emphasized ethnic particularity and suggested that the price of assimilation might result in humiliation and ridicule. When they moved their studio to Florida in 1938, they found themselves cut off from their roots in New York's Lower East Side and shortly thereafter faded from view, a footnote to film history (Holberg 10).

Woody Allen and Mel Brooks

Jewish comedians existed in films and on stage long before the appearance of Woody Allen and Mel Brooks. This point was evident in the "Jewish Comedy Then and Now" program hosted by Writers Bloc and the Casden Institute in spring 2002. Jewish comedians had dominated the standup comic scene of vaudeville, as well as the Catskill Mountains, and also were present on radio, notably entertainers such as Jack Benny and Eddie Cantor. With the advent of television, Jewish comedians such as Milton Berle,

Sid Caesar and Buddy Hackett seemed to be everywhere (Saposnik "These Serious..." 312). Until the 1960s, however, most of the comedians kept their ethnicity out of sight. This was true when Cantor or Benny appeared in films and continued through the 1960s with Jerry Lewis' antics on screen (Kaplan 20-24). It was understood, even without the ethnicity, that American Jewish comedians were using humor as a form of survival, as an outsider's voice of urban desperation (Saposnik "These Serious..." 315). By the 1970s, however, when Woody Allen and Mel Brooks were writing and directing their films, Jews in America were attending Ivy League colleges, joining firms that had previously shunned them, and generally moving freely *inside* the urban culture that dominated much of contemporary life.

Allen and Brooks responded to the new surroundings in America. They still saw themselves as outsiders because they were Jewish, but they now felt free to acknowledge it. That was their identity and the heart of their humor, and in contemporary America they felt no need for concealment. Critics have analyzed how Allen's anxiety and depression were connected to a desire to belong, while Brooks' manic behavior and fantasies of dealing with authority were attached to a Jew's fear and fury at Auschwitz and the Holocaust (Erens "You Could..." 52). It was argued that Allen and Brooks were in fact responding to the special burden of being Jewish in modern America (Erens "You Could..." 59).

The question is: Why did a non-Jewish mass audience relate to their humor? Irv Saposnik, executive director of the B'nai B'rith Hillel foundation in Madison, Wisconsin, speculates that "as more and more Americans began to call the city their home, they understood the meaning of being an outsider" (Saposnik "These Serious..." 313). They had come from other places and now found themselves coping as outsiders with modern urban life. Jews were the perfect guides. According to professor Patricia Erens, Woody Allen, by showing us how he is racked with guilt and suffering, makes Jews of us all. She quotes Allen: "You don't have to be Jewish to be traumatized, but it helps" (Erens "You Could..." 60).

Allen and Brooks had worked as writers for television's Sid Caesar and had performed standup comedy with an emphasis on Jewish neuroses and anxiety (Erens "You Could…" 52). The humor was zany and madcap, but it essentially highlighted the view of the outsider as victim—the man who wanted to belong. They used popular culture as the target for much of their humor, and this continued when they graduated to writing, directing and producing films: Allen in films such as *Annie Hall, Manhattan* and *Hannah and Her Sisters*; Brooks in *The Producers* and *Blazing Saddles*. The films served to develop their respectability (Saposnik "These Serious…" 314). The Jewish jokes and standup routines, brought to films in which Allen in particular served as a Jewish hero, helped legitimatize Jewish characters, giving them a weight equal to "WASP archetypes" (Saposnik "These Serious…" 317).

Almost from the beginning, their humor was filled with jokes about death. Allen's films delighted in the anxious pursuit of the denial of death: There was the death joke in *Annie Hall*, and concerns about death in *Interiors, Love and Death* and *Hannah and Her Sisters* (Erens "You Could…." 53-54). Brooks was wilder, more manic, bringing in Nazis, the inquisition and the fantasies of a Jewish mind that fended off death by keeping in constant motion. We see Orthodox Jewish prisoners in shackles in *History of the World, Part I* (Erens "You Could…" 58) and the antic "Springtime for Hitler" production at the center of *The Producers*. Erens quotes Allen in an explicit Jewish context: "Life is a concentration camp. You're stuck here, and there's no way out, and you can only rage impotently against your persecutors" (Erens "You Could…" 55). Erens believes that Allen and Brooks use comedy as a way of avoiding death and, eventually, of coming to terms with it. Brooks tames death "by turning his aggression against others," and Allen uses self-deprecation (Erens "You Could…" 58-59). In Allen, the roots of this belief are inextricably tied to his Jewish identity. Renée Curry has suggested that "his comedy is a truly labored art form, one that he has studied from childhood and one that continues to absorb him. Some viewers laugh in response to the schlemiel/little man and his hypochondria, his battle with despair, his victimization, his Jewish guilt, his neurosis, his displacement, his relationships with women, his physical dishevelment" (Curry 5).

Allen's films have proved a treasure trove for academic critics, and for a small but loyal segment of the movie-going public. Maurice Yacowar sees Allen using comedy as a way of engaging an audience (Curry 6). For Nancy Pogel, Allen's little man is a Chaplin-like figure caught partly in rebellion, partly in innocence (Curry 7). Some Jewish critics feel betrayed by him. Samuel H. Dresner, for instance, rebukes Allen for playing out the stereotype image of the Jew as victim and sees him as a despoiler of morality (Curry 17). Allen is obsessed with Jews, he believes, and Dresner cannot forgive him for depicting religious Jews as adulterers, lechers and hypocrites, and for lusting after Gentile women (Curry 191, 193). Mark E. Bleiweiss, meanwhile, concludes that Allen is merely complacent in his approach to Judaism but is concerned that he serves to undermine Jews and the Jewish tradition (Curry 17). We have all become outsiders, according to some of the critics. While many Jews may still see themselves as outsiders today, theirs is an internal vision. Acceptance from the majority group appears to have occurred either when Jews and Woody Allen and Mel Brooks were not looking, or precisely because their humor made Jewish comic figures and a Jewish point of view into "an American comic Everyman" (Saponick "These Serious..." 318).

Steven Spielberg

With the success of his 1993 film *Schindler's List*, Steven Spielberg is today seen as the premier Jewish American director. His commercially successful film collected a number of Academy Awards and was an enormously popular "media event, generating extensive discourse on the Holocaust and its mediation by popular culture in a way not seen in the United States since the 1978 NBC television series *Holocaust*" (Loshitzky 2). Spielberg's depiction of the Holocaust has managed to affect mainstream American culture and be successful overseas, in places such as Austria, Germany, Italy and Japan (Loshitzky 14). He has simultaneously created a tremendous "hit movie" and "transformed the image of the Holocaust...[throughout] the world" (Loshitzky 2-3).

Particularly important was the timing of the film, appearing just at the moment that the survivors were fading from the scene and taking with them personal recollections of the Holocaust. It could be viewed as "the victory of collective memory as transmitted by popular culture over a memory contested and debated by professional historians" (Loshitzky 3). Spielberg's great success in *Schindler's List*, for some critics, has been to affect the way we now understand the catastrophe that gripped the lives of Jews 60 years ago. He has responded as a Jewish American director, Americanizing the Holocaust, celebrating survival over death and symbolically transforming the "mourning over the six million Jews who perished in Europe...into a celebration of the 5 million Jews living in America today" (Loshitzky 4).

Nevertheless, the critical reception has not been universally positive. Some critics have argued that while Spielberg involves us intimately with the Shoah in all its horror, he has also perhaps desensitized us to the actual nightmare that occurred, by exploring an exception to the better-known events of history (Hoffman 2). Spielberg's film *Amistad* has been similarly cited as an exception to the history of slavery and the slave trade as we know it. It recounts the story of an uprising in 1839, when 53 Africans held in the ship's slave galley and marked for slavery in the New World rebelled and killed most of the crew before they landed in Montauk (Forman 37-38). These critics question whether Spielberg's *Schindler's List* will alter history, reshaping the dominant images of the Holocaust in the public mind (Loshitzky 2), and whether the relationship of cinematic events to what is internalized as personal history by the groups portrayed, may be detrimental in some cases (Forman 37-38).

Despite criticism that *Schindler's List* could mislead viewers by featuring Oskar Schindler's story, many saw the intrinsic educational value of Spielberg's film. The movie is believed to have "symbolically pass[ed] the torch from one generation to the next, reaffirming the role of generational identity in the symbolic memory culture of the Holocaust" (Loshitzky 4). *Schindler's List* also became a teaching tool in and outside the classroom. New Jersey's then-governor, Christie Todd Whitman, saw the movie and later signed a bill in 1994 mandating that all New Jersey schoolchildren were to be taught about genocide and the Holocaust. "Governor Whitman's response to the film as well as Spielberg's testifying before the American Congress, attest to the status that *Schindler's List* has already achieved in American historical consciousness. It has attainted the status of historical document, the final and undeniable proof…" (Loshitzky 5). By telling the story of Oskar Schindler, Spielberg opened up the opportunity for many other stories about the Holocaust to be told.

Spielberg's personal and professional investments after the making of *Schindler's List* also have contributed in important ways to the ability of future generations to make sense of the Shoah. With the founding and development of the Shoah Foundation and the Righteous Persons Foundation, Spielberg has used his influence to create organizations devoted to recording the past while providing for Jewish Americans' present and future.

The Shoah Visual History Foundation began in 1994 after the completion of *Schindler's List*. Its intent was to create "a resource so enduring that 50, 100, or even 500 years from now, people around the world will learn directly from survivors and witnesses about the atrocities of the Holocaust—what it means to survive and how our very humanity depends upon the practice of tolerance and mutual respect" (Tugend 20). The foundation employs interviewers in 57 countries and as of 2002 has collected 52,000 testimonies of survivors and others who were in concentration camps, hid during the Holocaust, lived under Nazi rule or rescued Nazi victims. Now entering a new phase of cataloguing the testimonies and developing the software to make the archives accessible all over the world, Spielberg himself is reminded why the foundation was established: "To affect one person at a time. To change a life in even the smallest way, so that they might stop and consider the consequences of their actions or choice. This is why the Shoah Foundation exists" (Tugend 20-21).

The foundation also has used its testimonies as a springboard for additional documentaries about aspects of the Holocaust never before shared. One of the films was 1999s *The Last Days,* which told the story of five Jewish survivors from Hungary, and was presented by Steven Spielberg and the Shoah Visual History Foundation. The feature-length documentary was honored with the Academy Award for Best Documentary Feature and was developed as a direct result of testimonies collected through the Shoah Foundation (Tugend 20).

"For a director like Spielberg [as for the American Jewish community at large], what matters is survival" (Loshitzky 4). Consequently, Spielberg completed *Schindler's List* and looked to the future. After developing an organization to preserve the past, he then provided and continues to provide opportunities for American Jews through the Righteous Persons Foundation he established in the fall of 1994. This foundation focuses on Jewish youth and young adults, encouraging Jewish learning. Tolerance within inter-group relationships is another focus of the organization. Using media and the arts to reach broad audiences and explore what it means to be a Jew is just one of the ways the foundation seeks to foster a Jewish American future (www.s2k.org/About/founding funders.html).

Changing Portraits

Over the past 50 years, life has changed dramatically for American Jews. Details of the Holocaust have helped rekindle feelings of Jewish identity, the evolution of the state of Israel has reinforced ethnic identification, and the huge increase of intermarriage—while blending the Jewish and non-Jewish population—has functioned as a threat to survival (Gabler "An Empire..." 6). These changes in life conditions and perception have been mirrored for Jewish Americans in portrayals and narratives of contemporary films, which in turn have reshaped the cultural life of most Americans (Gabler "An Empire..." 21-28).

None of the changes in film and television portrayals has been more significant, or more startling, than narratives about the Holocaust. America's relationship to it was distant, whereas

Europeans had a more intimate connection (Doneson 7). Nevertheless, such American films as *Schindler's List, Judgment at Nuremberg* and *The Diary of Anne Frank*, along with the television miniseries *Holocaust,* have been far more influential here and abroad than any European films on the Holocaust (Doneson 7). The Americanization of depictions of the Holocaust may have occurred partly because it became a metaphor for contemporary action, at times related to civil rights or even anti-war protests. These are all linked, for example, in the video segments of the Simon Wiesenthal's Holocaust Museum in Los Angeles. The appropriation of the Holocaust by American filmmakers serves in this sense as a reflection of history and a function of the needs perceived and desired by present-day society (Doneson 8). Jewish Americans, in the past, perceived themselves as passive, as victims; today there is a determination on the part of Jews in films to express ethnic pride and to change the earlier image. "The old Hollywood represented studio heads who were ashamed of being Jewish.... That has changed" said Marvin Hier, dean and founder of the Simon Wiesenthal Center (Wallenstein 52).

In addition, there has been added pressure on Hollywood producers from those who are guardians of the Holocaust. Survivor and Nobel Peace Prize winner Elie Wiesel initially opposed the idea of films about the Holocaust: The experience had been too horrific, and television and movies would only lead to banality. He had denounced the television miniseries *Holocaust* as soap opera, but then had been shocked to discover that a New York Times poll (later found inaccurate by researchers) had shown that 22 percent of American adults had doubts about the existence of the Holocaust. Better to establish the Holocaust as a cultural fact in the American landscape than worry about trivializing it, he concluded (Doneson 223).

Leon Wieseltier, the literary critic at the *New Republic* magazine, analyzed the dilemma over the Holocaust during an interview on the *Nightline* television program. "There is a sense, and the reception of Spielberg's film confirms this, in which one thing doesn't have reality in this culture until Hollywood says it does" (Doneson 229). A more skeptical view attributes the radical change to the commercial and Academy Award success of films such as *Life Is Beautiful* and *Schindler's List* (Wallenstein 52), whose grosses exceeded $229 million and $321 million respectively.

Hollywood's Jewish writers and producers in the last several decades have found themselves freer to explore cultural realities other than the Holocaust that may have been considered outside acceptable boundaries during the studio system enforced by the moguls. Recent films such as *Kissing Jessica Stein* and *Trembling Before G-d* feature characters and situations absent in earlier films. *Kissing Jessica Stein*, which tells the story of "a charming yet neurotic Jewish girl who falls in love with a woman" is, on one level, a film directed at a lesbian audience. But on another it is also a film about "desperation, experimentation, human connection, sexuality conformity and prejudice." (Toumarkine 2). It is modern urban Jewish humor touching on relationships and functioning "as a kind of 'Same Sex and the City'" (Toumarkine 3).

The documentary "Trembling Before G-d" poses a different kind of challenge by focusing on homosexuality in the Orthodox Jewish community, two highly particularized groups outside mainstream America. The film received a number of awards and broke a box office record in New York in October 2002 (Yahr 1), suggesting that the American audience's interests have widened and that gays and Orthodox Jewry are no longer taboo subjects for films.

The ease with which Jews now occupy the screen as actors and film characters apparently has removed some of the strictures against projecting negative images about or toward them. It has become the norm, for example, for Jewish actors (and others) to play Jewish characters in films, with Jews often marked as "intelligent, intellectual or rational" and therefore different, which is not always seen as a compliment (Weiner 2). The diversity and complexity of the characters and the films, moreover, have tended to shatter some of the earlier stereotypes. Leonard Nimoy has spoken persuasively about the Jewish attributes he brought to bear in his portrayal of the intellectual Vulcan, an outsider within the *Star Trek* family (Levitan 23-27). Sander L. Gilman, a psychiatrist, professor at the University of Illinois in Chicago, and guest lecturer at USC's Casden Institute, has written about the complex Jewish characters found in such diverse films as *The Last Tycoon*, directed by Elia Kazan and based on a novel by F. Scott Fitzgerald, director-actress Barbra Streisand's adaptation of Isaac Bashevis Singer's *Yentl,* and director Robert Redford's *Quiz Show* (Erens "The Jew..." 91). In a review of Gilman's book *Smart Jews* for *Society* magazine in 1998, critic Lauren Weiner singles out the author's observation that the television show *Northern Exposure* had a Gentile character remark, "Jews are smarter than everyone else because they are Jews" (Weiner 5). Gilman believes this view permeated popular culture in the 1990s (Weiner 4). It apparently is no longer forbidden to write or convey this in films and television, unlike Budd Schulberg's Hollywood experience with *What Makes Sammy Run*.

This far wider acceptance and response to Jewish roles in American films and television also has led to a growing number of Jewish film festivals, as well as documentary films that are Jewish autobiographies. The San Francisco Festival, which began in 1981, initiated the screening of documentaries, features and experimental films from around the world, all focused on Jewish themes or subjects. Since then it has proliferated, so that Jewish film festivals occur in many major cities and at colleges and universities (Kaufman 18). In recent years, as independent filmmakers have taken their work to general festivals, the Jewish film festivals have seen an increased interest in autobiographical documentaries. Alan Berliner's *Nobody's Business*, a 1996 portrait of the filmmaker's father, complete with military service, failed marriage and family life with Berliner and his sister, has won awards and prizes at major festivals worldwide. Berliner was also an Emmy award winner (twice) and appeared with his film at the Eye & Thou conference on Jewish Autobiography in Film and Video in 1998. The conference was co-sponsored by the Institute for the Study of Jews in American Life at USC, which is today the Casden Institute.

The Casden Institute has played a not inconsiderable role in the documentary field, along with partners such as New York

University, the Righteous Persons Foundation and the Jewish Filmmakers Forum of USC Hillel. Events such as Eye & Thou and the USC Jewish Student film festival, both of which went bicoastal recently, have attracted the interest of scholars and critics. The Jewish USC film festivals, for example, were conceptualized and brought to fruition with the help of professor Michael Renov, a USC School of Cinema-Television documentary film scholar and member of the Casden Institute Advisory Board. They included the participation of Kenneth Turan, film critic of *the Los Angeles Times*, Jeremy Kagan, visiting professor of cinema-television at USC, and Faye Ginsburg, director of the Center for Media, Culture and History at New York University. Some of the films that were featured were Alan Berliner's *The Sweetest Sound*, Peter Forgacs' *The Maelstrom*, Deborah Hoffman's *Complaints of a Dutiful Daughter* and Lynn Hershman's *The Electronic Diaries: First Person Plural*.

These events have been supplemented by special screenings of documentaries at the Casden Institute, such as the Feb. 2, 2001, showing of Mark Jonathan Harris' *Into The Arms of Strangers: Stories of the Kindertransport*. The documentary, which chronicled the lives of the children sent from Europe to England in the late 1930s in search of refuge from Nazi oppression, was narrated by Dame Judi Dench and was awarded an Academy Award. Harris, who also won an Oscar for his 1997 Holocaust documentary *The Long Way Home*, is a significant presence and resource at USC, where he is a professor at the School of Cinema-Television (http Amazon).

The flourishing of documentaries has been aided, in part, by the availability of less expensive digital equipment. It is now possible to tape and record with a camera that has built-in sound. The equipment is light and far less expensive than the camera and sound equipment that determined and limited documentary filmmaking in earlier decades. According to professor Michael Renov, documentaries have entered a new era. The breadth of attention they have received at film festivals and academic conferences and in studies and analyses, demonstrates they are no longer on the margins of film study. Given the blurring of the line between fiction and nonfiction media forms, "it makes sense that a broad range of specialized subfields should look to the documentary for its objects of study with a level of interest equal to that accorded fiction" (Gaines and Renov 317).

Conclusion

In this chapter, we have examined the evolving role of Jews in American film and discovered how Jewish filmmakers have gone from marginal outsiders to powerful forces in the industry.

As immigrants in the United States, Jews often found themselves unable to break into any industry successfully; these closed doors and the accompanying rejection provided significant challenges for the men who founded the movie industry. However, with the development of the nickelodeon came the opportunity for Jewish individuals to involve themselves in a new form of mass culture. While nickelodeons were not well-respected, they were not costly and therefore within economic reach. The Jews running the nickelodeons were thereby able to appeal to moviegoers by producing and filming stories reflecting struggles among generations and classes—experiences urban and immigrant audiences alike could appreciate.

We also examined how, in an era in which many cultures and characters were stereotyped, Jews were not. With the exception of the overbearing Jewish mother character, most scholars and critics find that film studios were diligent in keeping unflattering portrayals of Jews off the screen (Erens "The New..." 19).

The 1920s brought economic growth, which led to a desire for assimilation into American culture. This desire to be integrated in society was reflected in the absence of Jewish characters and stories on the screen. Blending in as Americans, in their professional and personal lives, appeared to take priority for the leaders of the film industry over directly associating their motion pictures with characteristics, or even an audience, that could be described as Jewish.

Hollywood continued to put Jewish characters and storytelling on the back burner from 1930 through World War II; however, this time it was for different reasons. Keeping Jewish characters off the screen continued until the breakup of the studio system. Only then were mainstream films such as *Yentl, Norma Rae* and others produced.

This chapter also investigated the role of anti-Semitism in the film industry. Some critics complained that Jewish Americans were controlling Hollywood, a claim that has since only partly waned. Other critics argued that Jewish minor characters were portrayed often as the moral center of a film, and that Jews were creating an idealized version of themselves. The films were viewed as a form of propaganda. Criticism aside, it is true that new directors, actors, producers and writers have emerged with a newfound commitment to their Jewishness and reflect that in their film work.

We looked at several individuals who made significant contributions to their industry as Jewish American filmmakers or industry professionals. Early on, the Fleischer brothers, Max and Dave, embraced their Jewish identity during the silent age of film. Because they did so, they met with opposition from the studios and lost in their competition with Walt Disney. Woody Allen and Mel Brooks tested the boundaries of their Jewish identity, bringing a comedic edge to significant Jewish issues from the Holocaust to less-than-flattering depictions of Jewish characters. Later, Steven Spielberg created *Schindler's List*, a depiction of the Holocaust that affected American mainstream culture and provided an opportunity for developing the largest archive of Holocaust survivor testimonies.

This chapter also shows the evolving themes in Jewish filmmaking throughout history. From the debate over depictions of the Holocaust in film to documentary filmmakers exploring their roots to emerging stories about new Jewish characters focusing on youth and ethnicity, it becomes clear how widely Jewish filmmakers have embraced the many different facets of their Jewish identity. Costs and distribution still pose a barrier. But the presence of Jewish filmmakers' works in festivals and at venues provided by such institutions as the Casden Institute and the Simon Wiesenthal Center, as well as the availability of lower-cost, lightweight equipment, demonstrate how the documentary film field has turned around. It is now drawing the attention of many young filmmakers and academics who see a great area for art and exploration in the medium. With leading Jewish filmmakers further asserting their identity, and Jewish film festivals acknowledging and encouraging younger Jewish filmmakers, we can expect a further flowering of Jewish storytelling in this next decade.

The story of the Jewish contribution to American cinema, a story of challenges, achievement and hope for the future, seems a fitting conclusion to this second volume. In the process of documenting the rise from immigrant outsiders to industry movers and shakers, the emerging Jewish role in American film has its parallels in the broader experience of Jews in American life. On the one hand, Jews in the film industry have throughout the years faced the challenges of intense scrutiny, censorship and anti-Semitism, as well as the natural shifts in loyalties and priorities found in the American political climate of the day. At the same time, increased acceptance, power and wealth have brought a new sense of responsibility.

As in other fields we have discussed in this volume, the unique position of being a minority with some degree of authority has led American Jewish filmmakers to think seriously about where this places them in the scheme of American life. The recent surge in critically acclaimed Jewish-themed movies and film festivals suggests that this self-investigation is proving fruitful, both artistically and commercially. With success, however, has come a newfound recognition: Namely that the contributions of Jews to American film will both significantly inform the popular culture of today and make a lasting impact on the medium for years to come. That has become a new and unexpected responsibility.

Works Cited

Ackerman, Seth. "Al-Aqsa Intifada and the U.S. Media." *Journal of Palestine Studies* 30 (2001): 61-74.

Adler Marks, Marlene. "Beyond Stem Cells." *The Jewish Journal of Greater Los Angeles* 27 July (2001).

Agam, Yaacov. *Contemporary Artists,* 4th ed. St. James Press, 1996.

Al-Marayati, Salam. "Defining Terrorism for America: Jewish and Muslim Cases and Their Readings by the American Public." *CCAR Journal* (2000): 29-40.

Amazon.com. Rev. of *Into the Arms of Strangers: Stories of the Kindertransport*. Director Mark Jonathan Harris. 11 June 2002 URL: http://www.amazon.com/exec/obidos/ASIN/B00005MEPJ/qid=1023993654/sr=1 1/ref=sr_1_1/102-6668301-4088929

Amazon.com. Rev. of *The Haunted Smile*, by Lawrence Epstein. 17 June 2002 URL: http://www.amazon.com/exec/obidos/ASIN/1891620711/qid=1023999393/sr=8 1/ref=sr_8_1/102-6668301-4088929

Amazon.com. Rev. of *Undue Risk: Secret State Experiments on Humans*, by Jonathan Moreno. 22 May 2002 URL: http://www.amazon.com/exec.obidos/tg/stores/detail/-/books/0716731428/revies/102 5771660-2333733

Ansen, David. Rev. of *Kissing Jessica Stein*. "Jessica Delivers: Cute Package, No Labels." *Newsweek* 18 March (2002): 60.

"A Survivor's Story." 11 June 2002 URL: http://www.survivorstory.com/film.html

Auerbach, Jerold. "Are We One?: American Jews and Israel." *Midstream* January (1998): 20-23.

Avisar, Ilan. *Screening the Holocaust*. Bloomington: Indiana University Press, 1988.

Baigell, Matthew. "Max Weber's Jewish Paintings." *American Jewish History* 88 (2000): 341-360.

Baigell, Matthew and Heyd, Milly, eds. *Complex Identities: Jewish Consciousness in Modern Art*. Rutgers: Rutgers University Press, 2001.

Belitsky, Helen. "The Ties That Might Not Bind." *Moment* June (1999): 36-38.

Bernheimer, Kathryn. *The 50 Greatest Jewish Movies*. Seacaucus: Carol Publishing Group, 1998.

Bernstein, Adam. "Filmmaker Billy Wilder Dies." *The Washington Post* 29 March (2001).

Birnbaum, Milton. Rev. of *In Search of American Jewish Culture*, by Stephen Whitfield. *Midstream* 46 September (2000): 42.

Bohlin, Ray. "The Controversy Over Stem Cell Research." *Probe Ministries* (2001) 3 May 2002. URL: http://www.probe.org/docs/stemcells.html

Bourguignon, Erika. Rev. of *Smart Jews: The Construction of the Image of Jewish Superior Intelligence*, by Sander Gilman. *The Antioch Review* 55 (1997): 377.

Brackman, Harold. "The Attack on 'Jewish Hollywood': A Chapter in the History of Modern American Anti-Semitism." *Modern Judaism* 20 (2000): 1-19.

Brackman, Nicole. "Who Is a Jew? The American Jewish Community in Conflict With Israel." *Journal of Church and State* 41 (1999): 795-822.

Breitowitz, Yitzchok. "AIDS: A Jewish Perspective." *Jewish Law* (2001). 3 May 2002 URL: http://www.jlaw.com/Articles/aids.html

Breitowitz, Yitzchok. "The Brain Death Controversy in Jewish Law." *Jewish Law* (2001). 3 May 2002 URL: http://www.jlaw.com/Articles/brain.html

Broyde, Michael. "Cloning People and Jewish Law: A Preliminary Analysis." *Jewish Law* (2001). 3 May 2002 URL: http://www.jlaw.com/Articles/cloning.html

Burtt, Shelley. "Which Babies?" *Tikkun* 16 (2001): 45.

Chazan, Barry, and Cohen, Steven M. "What We Know About American Jewish Youth and Young Adults: Some Implications for Birthright Israel." *Journal of Jewish Communal Services* 77 (2000): 76-82.

Chen, Gilad. "Israeli Youth Discover Their Judaism in America." *Moment* February (1999): 54-55.

Clarens, Carlos. "Mogul—That's a Jewish Word." *Film Comment* July/August (1981): 34-36.

Cohen, Richard. "Exhibiting History or History in a Showcase." *Jewish History* 12 (1998): 97-112.

Cohen, Steven M. "Jewish Continuity Over Judaic Content: The Moderately Affiliated American Jew." *The Americanization of the Jews*, eds. Robert M. Seltzer and Norman J. Cohen. New York and London: New York University Press, 1995. 395-416.

Cooper, Abraham, and Brackman, Harold. "Through a Glass, Darkly: Durban and September 11th." *Midstream* November (2001): 2-8.

Cooperman, Alan. "2 Jewish Groups Back Therapeutic Cloning." *The Washington Post Online* 13 March (2001).

Curry, Renee. *Perspectives on Woody Allen*. New York: G.K. Hall, 1996.

Darvick, Debra. "Tapping Into Jewish Ways to Get Involved." *Moment* April (2000): 66-71, 88.

Davis, Sally Ogle. "Television Jews: How Jewish Is Too Jewish?" *The Jewish Journal of Greater Los Angeles* 7 September (2001).

Doneson, Judith. *The Holocaust in American Film*. Syracuse: Syracuse University Press, 2002.

Dorff, Elliot. " 'Heal Us, Lord and We Shall Be Healed': The Role of Hope and Destiny in Jewish Bioethics." *Judaism* 48 (1999): 149-165.

Duskin Feldman, Ruth. "Stem Cell Research: A Humanistic Jewish Perspective." *Humanistic Judaism*: 20 (2002): 42-46.

Eisenberg, Daniel. "Stem Cell Research in Jewish Law." *Jewish Law* 2001. 30 April 2002 URL: http://www.jlaw.com/Articles/ stemcellres.html

Elwell, Sue Levi. "New Haggadot Ask Fresh Questions." *Forward* 22 March (2002).

Erens, Patricia. *The Jew in American Cinema*. Bloomington: Indiana University Press, 1984.

Erens, Patricia. "You Could Die Laughing: Jewish Humor and Film." *East-West Film Journal* 2 (1987): 50-62.

Fischel, Jack. "The Road to September 11th." *Midstream* February/ March (2002): 7-8.

Flynn, Michael. Rev. of *Undue Risk: Secret State Experiments on Humans,* by Jonathan Moreno. *Bulletin of the Atomic Sciences* 55 (1999): 58-65.

Forman, Seth. "Amistad, Schindler: Black and Jewish Identity." *Midstream* September/October (1998): 37-38.

Foxman, Abraham. "Blaming Jews for 9/11 Must Stop." Editorial. *New York Daily News* 27 November (2001).

Freedman, Benjamin. *Duty and Healing: Foundations of Jewish Bioethics*. New York: Routledge, 1999.

Freudenheim, Tom. "Museum of Jewish Heritage—A Living Memorial to the Holocaust." *Curator* 40 (1997): 296-300.

Freudenheim, Tom. "The Obligations of the Chosen: Jewish Museums in a Politically Correct World." *European Judaism* 34 (2001): 80-90.

Friedman, Lester. "The Conversion of the Jews." *Film Comment* 17 July/August (1981): 39-48.

Friedman, Lester. *Hollywood's Image of the Jew*. New York: Frederick Ungar Publishing, 1982.

Friedman, Lester. *The Jewish Image in American Film*. Seacaucus: Citadel Press, 1987.

Friedman, Lester. *Unspeakable Images: Ethnicity and the American Cinema.* Chicago: University of Illinois Press, 1991.

"From Memory to Museums." *National Foundation for Jewish Culture* 29 May 2002 URL: http://www.jewishculture.org/1997/memorymuseums.htm

Gabler, Neal. *An Empire of Their Own: How the Jews Invented Hollywood.* New York: Doubleday, 1988.

Gabler, Neal. "The Jewish Problem." *American Film* 13 July/August (1988): 37-44.

Gaines, Jane and Renov, Michael. *Collecting Visible Evidence.* Minneapolis: University of Minnesota Press, 1999.

Gay, Peter. "Is There a Jewish Way of Holding a Paintbrush?" *Forward* 26 April (2002).

Geiderman, Joel Martin. "Ethics Seminars: Physician Complicity in the Holocaust: Historical Review and Reflections on Emergency Medicine in the 21st Century, Part I." *Academic Emergency Medicine* 9 (2002): 223-231.

Geldman, Ardie. "The Growing Gap Between American Jews and Israel: Two Views." *Journal of Jewish Communal Service* 78 (2001): 32-40.

Girgus, Sam. *The Films of Woody Allen.* Cambridge: Cambridge University Press, 1993.

Goodwin, George. "More Than a Laughing Matter: Cartoons and Jews." *Modern Judaism* 21 (2001): 146-174.

Gordis, David, and Ben Horin, Yoav, eds. *Jewish Identity in America.* New York: KTAV Publishing House, 1991.

Grant, Lisa. "Planned and Enacted Curriculum Stories on a Congregational Israel Trip." *Conservative Judaism* 53 (2001): 63-81.

Grant, Lisa. "The Role of Mentoring in Enhancing Experience of a Congregational Israel Trip." *Journal of Jewish Education* 67 (2001): 46-60.

Grossman, Lawrence. "Transformation Through Crisis: The American Jewish Committee and the Six-Day War." *American Jewish History* 86 (1998): 27-54.

Grossman, Naomi. "The Gay Orthodox Underground." *Moment* April (2001): 55-60, 95-97.

Grossman, Rafael. "9-11 and Anti-Semitism." *Christian Action for Israel* 15 May 2002 URL: http://christianactionforisrael.org/antiholo/911.html

Gruenbaum Fax, Julie. "Challenging the Myth." *The Jewish Journal of Greater Los Angeles* 7 April (2000).

Halkin, Hillel. "The Return of Anti-Semitism." *Commentary* 113 (2002): 30-36.

Hazony, David. "Israel, America, And the War on Terror." Editorial. *Azure.* 12 (2002): 13-26.

Healy, John. "An Artful Way to Develop Character." *Norwalk* February 2002.

Helprin, Mark. "What Israel Must Now Do to Survive." *Commentary* 112 (2001): 25-28.

Herman, Felicia. "Hollywood, Nazism, and the Jews, 1933-41." *American Jewish History* 89 (2001): 61-89.

Hirschberg, Peter. "Be Fruitful and Multiply and Multiply and Multiply." *The Jerusalem Report.com* (1998).

Hoberman, J. "Yiddish Transit." *Film Comment* July/August (1981): 36-38.

Hoffman, Warren. Rev. of *In Search of American Jewish Culture*, by Stephen Whitfield. "Bagels with a Schmear of Culture." *Judaism* 50 Spring (2001): 249.

Holberg, Amelia. "Betty Boop: Yiddish Film Star." *American Jewish History* 87 (1999): 291.

"The Holy Land: David Roberts—Dead Sea Scrolls—House of David Inscription." *Bowers Museum Past Exhibitions.* 29 May 2002 URL: http://www.bowers.org/holyland.html

Intrator, Sam and Rosov, Wendy. "Sustaining the Work of Creation: A Exploration of Jewish Environmental Education." *Journal of Jewish Education.* 64 (1998): 102-114.

"Jewish Museums." *National Foundation for Jewish Culture.* 29 May 2002 URL: http://www.jewishculture.org/1998/cajm98.htm

Jochnowitz, George. "Why Terrorism?" *Midstream* February/March 2002: 9-10.

Kaplan, Arie. "Wizards of Wit: How Jews Revolutionized Comedy in America, Part I: 1950-1969." *Reform Judaism* Winter (2001): 19-28.

Karatnycky, Adrian, and Puddington, Arch. "The Human-Rights Lobby Meets Terrorism." *Commentary* 113 (2002): 28-31.

Kaufman, Deborah, and Plotkin, Janis, eds. *A Guide to Films Featured in the Jewish Film Festival.* n.p.: n.p., n.d.

Kass, Leon, and Callahan, Daniel. "Ban Stand Redux." *Daily Express* April 6 (2001).

Klagsbrun, Francine. "McCarthy, All Over Again?" *Moment* April (2002): 30-31.

Klaidman, Daniel. "A Murder Most Foul: Daniel Pearl Was Brutally Butchered By His Captors. How the United States Plans to Avenge His Death." *Newsweek* 4 March (2002).

Kriesberg, Louis. "Negotiating the Partition of Palestine and Evolving Israeli-Palestinian Relations." *The Brown Journal of World Affairs* 7 (2000): 63-80.

Kurtzman, Daniel. "Ethicists Relieved by Court Ruling on Suicides." *Jewish News of Greater Phoenix.* 15 May 2002 URL: http://www.jewishaz.com/jewishnews/970704/ethicist.shtml

Lambert, Miriam. "From New York to Jerusalem." *American Prospect* 11 (2000).

Lapin, Daniel. "Misrepresenting the Holocaust." *The American Enterprise* 10 (1999).

Lee, Sander. *Woody Allen's Angst: Philosophical Commentaries on His Serious Films.* London: McFarland & Company, 1997.

Letran, Vivian. "Ancient Dispatches From the Holy Land." *The Los Angeles Times* 7 October 2001.

Letran, Vivian. "Teens Cancel Out on Israel." *The Los Angeles Times* 11 May 2002.

Levin, Mark, and Birnbaum, Ira. "Jewish Bioethics?" *Journal of Medicine and Philosophy* 25 (2000): 469-484.

Levitan, Sonia. "The Vulcan Is a Real Jew." *Reform Judaism* Spring (1998): 22-27.

Lewis, Samuel. "The United States and Israel: Evolution of an Unwritten Alliance." *The Middle East Journal* 53 (1999): 364-378.

Lipman, Steve. "America's Jewish Laugh Track." *The Jewish Week* 26 November (2001).

Litvak, Richard. "Erev Rosh Hashanah U'vchen: And Therefore Sanctify Life." *Judaism* 50 (2001): 398-405.

Lopate, Phillip. "A Bouquet of Grief and Sex." *Film Comment* November/ December (2001): 67-70.

Loshitzky, Yosefa, ed. *Spielberg's Holocaust*. Indianapolis: Indiana University Press, 1997.

Lowenstein, Lael. Rev. of *Kissing Jessica Stein*. *Variety* 7 May (2001): 62.

Ludmer-Gliebe, Susan. "3,400 Years of Treasures." *Reform Judaism* Spring (2001): 42-44.

Magnes Museum. Curatorial Statement. "Ben Katchor: Picture—Stories." 29 May 2002 URL: http://www.jmsf.org/exhibitions/benkatchor/katchor_curatorial.html

Maguire, Daniel. "Listen to the Many Voices on 'When Life Begins.' " *The Los Angeles Times* 6 August 2001.

Maiman, William. "Witnessing History." *TCI* 32 (1998): 48-49.

Maisel, Louis Sandy, and Forman, Ira, eds. *Jews in American Politics*. Lanham: Rowman and Littlefield Publishers, 2001.

"Making a Difference in a Difficult Year—Leon Kass." *Forward* (2001). 23 May 2002 URL: http://www.forward.com/issues/2001/01.11.09/forwardfifty.html

Marantz, Haim, ed. *Judaism & Education: Essays in Honor of Walter I. Ackerman.* Beer-Sheeva: Ben Gurion University Press, 1998.

Mart, Michelle. "Constructing a Universal Ideal: Anti-Semitism, American Jews, and the Founding of Israel." *Modern Judaism* 20 (2000): 181-208.

Messikomer, Carla, Fox, Renee, and Swazey, Judith. "The Presence and Influence of Religion in American Bioethics." *Perspectives in Biology and Medicine* 44 (2001): 485-509.

Meyer Jr., William. "An American 'Precedent'? Propaganda in American Movies: The Case of the Hollywood Jews." *Literature-Film Quarterly* 27 (1999): 271-281.

Miller, Martin. "Life Support: The Haunted Smile." *Post-Gazette.com* 30 April (2002).

Mirvish, Adrian. "Suicide Bombers, Authoritarian Minds, and the Denial of Others." *Judaism* 50 (2001): 387-397.

Moore, Deborah Dash, and Troen, S. Ilan, eds. *Divergent Jewish Cultures: Israel and America.* Cambridge: Yale University Press, 2001.

Myers, David N. "The Return of Big Brother?" *Jewish Journal of Greater Los Angeles* October 18 (2002).

"Nearly $2 Million in 9/11 Aid Disbursed From United Jewish Communities Emergency Fund." Press Release. *United Jewish Communities* 12 December 2001.

Newman, Louis. "Talking Ethics With Strangers: A View From Jewish Traditions." *Journal of Medicine and Philosophy* 18 (1993): 549-567.

Newman, Louis. "Jewish Theology and Bioethics." *Journal of Medicine and Philosophy* 17 (1992): 309-327.

Nichols, Mary. *Reconstructing Woody.* New York: Rowman & Littlefield, 1998.

Nimoy, Leonard. "So Human." *Reform Judaism* Fall (1999): 26-28.

Nordlinger, Jay. "Rude Awakenings." *National Review Online* July (2002). 2 July 2002. URL: http//www.nationalreview.com/ 15July02/nordlinger071502.asp

Novak, David. "Bioethics and the Contemporary Jewish Community." *The Hastings Center Report* 20 (1990).

Novak, David. Rev. of *Matters of Life and Death: A Jewish Approach to Modern Medical Ethics*, by Elliot N. Dorff. *First Things* November (1999): 66.

Ockman, Carol. "Too Jewish? Challenging Traditional Identities." *Artforum International*. 35 (1996): 106-108.

Olin, Margaret. *The Nation Without Art: Examining Modern Discourses on Jewish Art*. Nebraska: The University of Nebraska Press, 2001.

Perlmutter, Ruth. "The Melting Pot and the Humoring of America: Hollywood and the Jew." *Film Reader* 5 (1982): 247-256.

Pfefferman, Naomi. "Messing Up Stereotypes." *Jewish Journal of Greater Los Angeles* 3 May (2002).

Plaut, Steven. "The Limits to Unthinkability." *Jewish Magazine* 24 September (2001).

Podhoretz, Norman. "How to Win World War IV." *Commentary* 113 (2002): 19-29.

Popper, Frank. *Agam*, 3rd. Rev. Ed. New York: H.N. Abrams, 1990. 3 February 2003 URL: http://www.agam.net/ownwords/lifestory4.html

Quart, Leonard. "The Triumph of Assimilation: Ethnicity, Race and the Jewish Moguls." *Cineaste* 18 (1991): 8-11.

Reimer, Joseph. *Succeeding at Jewish Education: How One Synagogue Made it Work*. Philadelphia: Jewish Publication Society, 1997.

Reisman, Bernard. *The Jewish Experiential Book: The Quest for Jewish Identity*. New York: KTAV Publishing House, 1979.

Reisner, Avram. "Curiouser and Curiouser: Teshuvah on Genetic Engineering." *Conservative Judaism* 52 (2000): 59-72.

Ritterband, Paul. "Modern Times and Jewish Assimilation." *The Americanization of the Jews*. Robert M. Seltzer, and Norman J. Cohen, eds. New York and London: New York University Press, 1995. 377-394.

Rogin, Michael. *Blackface, White Noise*. Berkeley: University of California Press, 1996.

Rolnick, Josh. "Saving a Remnant." *Moment* February (2001): 41.

Ross, Steven. *Working-Class Hollywood*. Princeton: Princeton University Press, 1998.

Samber, Sharon. "Cloning Controversy Multiplies." *Jewish Journal of Greater Los Angeles* 17 August (2001).

Samber, Sharon. "For Jews, Stem Cell Debate Still in Embryonic Stage." *Jewish Bulletin News* 27 July (2001).

Samber, Sharon. "Jewish Groups on Stem Cell Debate." *Jewish Journal of Greater Los Angeles* July 27 (2001).

Samberg, Joel. "Jewish Moms in the Movies." *Moment* October (2000): 63-65, 86.

Saposnik, Irving. "Jolson, Judy, and Jewish Memory." *Judaism* 50 (2001): 410-425.

Saposnik, Irving. "These Serious Jests: American Jews and Jewish Comedy." *Judaism* 47 (1983): 311-320.

Satel, Sally, and Stolba, Christine. "Who Needs Medical Ethics?" *Commentary* 11 February (2001): 37-38.

Schein, Jeffrey, and Staub, Jacob, eds. *Creative Jewish Education: A Reconstructionist Perspective*. Chappaqua, N.Y.: Reconstructionist Rabbinical College Press.

Schickel, Richard. Rev. of *Kissing Jessica Stein*. "Rules of Engagement: Finding Modern Love in Some Surprising Places." *Time* 25 March (2002): 70-71.

Schoenfeld, Gabriel. "Could September 11 Have Been Averted?" *Commentary* 112 (2001): 21-29.

Schoenfeld, Gabriel, and Critics. "Counterterrorism Before September 11." *Commentary* 113 (2002): 12-16.

Segal, Daniel. "Can You Tell a Jew When You See One? Or Thoughts on Meeting Barbra/Barbie at the Museum." *Judaism* 48 (1999): 234-241.

Seltzer, Robert M., and Cohen, Norman J., eds. *The Americanization of the Jews*. New York: New York University Press, 1995.

Shannon, Phil. Rev. of *Undue Risk: Secret Experiments on Humans*, by Jonathan Moreno. *Green Left Weekly* 447 (2001).

Silverman, Adam. "Just War, Jihad, and Terrorism: A Comparison of Western and Islamic Norms for the Use of Political Violence." *Journal of Church and State* 44 (2002): 73-92.

"The Skirball: Everyone's Jewish Museum." *National Foundation for Jewish Culture*. 29 May 2002 URL: http://www.jewishculture.org/jen.SP96-3.htm

Soll, Jennifer. "Skirball's Cultural Mandate: Industry Active in Events Celebrating Jewish-American Life." *Variety* 373 16-22 November (1998).

Soussloff, Catherine. "Projecting Culture: Jewish Art Historians and the History of Art History." *Judaism* 49 (2000): 352-357.

Soussloff, Catherine, ed. *Jewish Identity in Modern Art History*. Berkeley: University of California Press, 1999.

Spinowitz, Moshe, and Steinberg, Avi. "Dual Identities." Editorial. *The Harvard Mosaic* 29 (2002): 3.

Starger, Steven. "Identity, Politics, Art and the Museum: Questions, but Few Answers, About the Place of Culture Identity in the Museum." *Art New England* 23 (2001/2002).

Stukin, Stacie. Rev. of *Kissing Jessica Stein*. "How the Other Half Laughs." *The Advocate* 19 March (2002): 52-53.

"Tak for Alt: Survival of a Human Spirit," entry in *Internet Movie Database*. 11 June 2002 URL: http://us.imdb.com/Title?0228919

Tenzer, Heather. "In Vitro Fertilization—Kosher or Not?" *Moment* (2001). 23 May 2002 URL: http://www.momentmag.com/archive/oct99/extra3.html

Terris, Bruce. "Common Sense in Profiling." *Midstream* February/March 2002: 11-12.

Tickton Schuster, Diane and Aron, Isa. "What Congregations Need to Know About the Adult Learner." *Reform Judaism* Summer (1998): 43-46.

Toumarkine, Doris. Rev. of *Kissing Jessica Stein*. *Film Journal International* March (2002): 98-99.

Troy, Gil. "Birthright Israel: Why I Was Wrong." *Moment* August (2000): 54-57, 88-91.

Troy, Gil. "Reviving Zionism." *Moment* February (2002): 50-54.

Tugend, Tom. "Tackling the Future." *Jewish Journal of Greater Los Angeles* 6 December (2002): 20-21.

Wallenstein, Andrew. "Shoah Business." *Moment* April (2002): 51-55, 76-77.

Weiner, Lauren. Rev. of *Smart Jews: The Construction of the Image of Jewish Superior Intelligence,* by Sander Gilman. *Society* 35 (1998): 2.

Wertheimer, Jack. "The Disaffections of American Jews." *Commentary* 105 (1998).

Whitfield, Stephen. *In Search of American Jewish Culture.* Hanover, New Hampshire: Brandeis University Press, 1999.

"Why Jewish Medical Ethics?" *The Institute for Jewish Medical Ethics.* 15 May 2002 URL: http://www.ijme.org/Content/Why/Steinberg.htm

Yacobi, Diana. "Jewish Education at the Frontline: A New Vision for the Twenty First Century." *Journal of Jewish Education* 66 (2001): 30-40.

Yahr, Harriette. "Gay Orthodox Jews in the Movies." *Tikkun* 17 January/February (2002).

Zelon, Helen. "Camp Comeback." *Moment* February (2000): 64-67, 84-85, 95.

Zoloth, Laurie. *Health Care and the Ethics of Encounter.* Chapel Hill: The University of North Carolina Press, 1999.

Zoloth-Dorfman, Laurie. "Research With Human Embryonic Stem Cells: Ethical Considerations." *The Hastings Center Report* March/April (1999): 31-36.

About the Authors

Barry Glassner is the Myron and Marian Casden Director of the Casden Institute for the Study of the Jewish Role in American Life and a professor of Sociology at the University of Southern California. Professor Glassner was chair of the Department of Sociology for six years prior to his directorship. Before coming to USC, he served as chair of Sociology at the University of Connecticut and Syracuse University. Professor Glassner has authored four books and co-authored or edited six books; his research papers have been published in leading scholarly journals.

Hilary Taub Lachoff is the Assistant Director of the Casden Institute for the Study of the Jewish Role in American Life at the University of Southern California. She has a B.A. from the University of Judaism and an M.A. from Vanderbilt University, both in the field of psychology. Ms. Lachoff has authored, co-authored or edited several training manuals, scholarly works and research papers. Her work has been published in *Science*.

Gene Lichtenstein is a journalist in Los Angeles, California. He started *The Jewish Journal* in 1985 and was editor of the weekly newspaper for 15 years. He has been a reporter and foreign correspondent on the staff of *The Economist of London*, and an editor/writer with *The New York Sunday Times*. His work has appeared in *The New York Times Sunday Magazine*, *Atlantic, Jewish Social Studies, Fortune, Esquire, Jerusalem Report, Forward, LA Weekly* and the *Los Angeles Times*. Mr. Lichtenstein was a Senior Research Associate at MIT, where he directed a number of educational research projects; a visiting professor at Northwestern University; and an adjunct professor at Berkeley, Columbia and USC.

Index